Updated 2024

Egyptian Alphabetical Letters of Creation Cycle

Moustafa Gadalla

CONTENTS

PART III :THE ORDERLY MANIFESTATION PHASE/
ENNEAD

1

ABOUT THE AUTIIOR

Moustafa Gadalla is an Egyptian-American independent Egyp-tologist who was born in Cairo, Egypt in 1944. He holds a Bache-lor of Science degree in civil engineering from Cairo University.

From his early childhood, Gadalla pursued his Ancient Egyptian roots with passion, through continuous study and research. Since 1990, he has dedicated and concentrated all his time to researching and writing.

Gadalla is the author of twenty-two published internationally acclaimed books about the various aspects of the Ancient Egypt-ian history and civilization and its influences worldwide. In addition he operates a multimedia resource center for accurate, educative studies of Ancient Egypt, presented in an engaging, practical, and interesting manner that appeals to the general pub-lic.

He was the Founder of Tehuti Research Foundation which was later incorporated into the multi-lingual Egyptian Wisdom Center (https://www.egyptianwisdomcenter.org) in more than ten languages.The website also includes another ongoing activity; his creation and production of performing arts projects such as the Isis Rises Operetta, Horus The Initiate Operetta; Egyptian Goddesses Operetta; and a few more other productions to follow.

2

PREFACE

The Ancient Egyptians considered the letters to be elemental, basic things in a very real sense. For the Stoics, it appears that language was not simply modeled after the physical world but belonged to it part and parcel. It was customary among the Egyptians to identify the letters of the alphabet (and with them the individual sounds of speech) as stoicheia literally physical particles. Throughout Egyptian history, the alphabet was invested with very real mundane significance. To them, letters are things not pictures of things.

This book focus on the relationship between the sequence of the creation cycle and the Egyptian ABGD alphabets. Such an orderly scientific sequence was expressed eloquently in poetic stanzas—which were called (lunar) mansions—for each letter and the cosmic creation role of each letter/mansion in the creation cycle. This very exact information was repeated later in Sufi (and other) references.

Creation is the actualization of divinity through a process of linguistic auto-representation. Creation and revelation amount to the same thing.

It is the aim of this book to provide such an exposition one which, while based on sound scholarship, will present the issues in language comprehensible to non specialist readers. Technical terms have been kept to a minimum. These are explained, as non-technically as possible, in the glossary. This book is divided into five parts containing a total of 35 chapters.

Part I. Egyptian Alphabetical Letters of Creation Cycle *has four chapters:*

Chapter 1: **Historical Deception of the (Ancient) Egyptian Linguistics** will clarify the intended confusion that hides the alphabetical form of writing in Ancient Egypt as the archetype of all languages throughout the world.

Chapter 2: **The Principles and Principals of Creation** covers the basic components of the creation cycle in the Ancient Egyptian accounts..

Chapter 3: **The Cosmic Manifestation of the Egyptian Alphabets** covers the natural, orderly progression of the emanated divine energy and its manifestation in the monthly lunar mansion changes and the correlations between the sequence of the ABGD letters and their numerical values.

Chapter 4: **The Three Primary Phases of the Creation Cycle** covers the nature of the creation cycle, consisting of three phases as found in the Ancient Egyptian accounts and later on duplicated in Sufi (and other) writings.

Part II. The Conceiving Phase/Ennead *has ten chapters—5 through 14:*

Chapter 5: **The Theme of the First Phase/Ennead** covers the theme of the First Phase/Ennead (1-9 'A' -'T.') as the objectification of a circumscribed area of undifferentiated energy/matter wherein the world will be manifested. It consists of the establishment of order and the co-factors of life forms as the foundation for the world. Phase One consists basically of three consecutive groups; each of which consists of 3 stages/letters/numbers.

Chapters 6 through 14 **cover the first nine letters**—each covering their role in the Creation Cycle, their sequence significance, their sound and writing form significance, numerical significance and their names and meanings, as well as their peculiar properties and nature/impact/influence.

Part III. The Orderly Manifestation Phase/Ennead *has ten chapters—15 through 24:*

Chapter 15: **The Theme of the Second Phase/Ennead** covers the theme of the Second Phase/Ennead, the orderly manifestation of creation. This Second Phase deals with the creation of the noumenal and phenomenal planes, the two grand subdivisions of the manifested world. The letters of this Phase are therefore arranged in two groups of four letters, and the middle letter 'N' overlaps the two planes:

'Y', 'K', 'L', 'M'   'N'   'S', '<u>A</u>.' , 'F', '<u>S</u>.'

Chapters 16 through 24 **cover the second nine letters**—each reviewing the same topics as in the prior group of nine letters.

Part IV. The Reunification Phase/Ennead *has ten chapters—25 through 34:*

Chapter 25 **covers the theme of the Third Phase/Ennead** which is the Ascending and Reunification Phase that leads to a NEW Alpha—Heru-Akhti of The Two Horizons.

Chapters 26 through 34 **cover the third nine letters**—each reviewing same topics as in the other two groups of nine letters.

Part V Being chapter 35 covers the 28th Mansion/Letter 'Gh' representing The New Alpha.

To learn about the linguistic features [words and sentences formations, etc.] of the Egyptian Alphabetical language, refer to other books by same author namely:

1. The Ancient Egyptian Universal Writing Modes

2. The Musical Aspects of The Ancient Egyptian Vocalic Language

See more details of these and other books at end of the book under TRF Publications.

Moustafa Gadalla

3

STANDARDS AND TERMINOLOGY

---

1. The Ancient Egyptian word, neter, and its feminine form netert, have been wrongly (and possibly intentionally) translated to 'god' and 'goddess' by almost all academicians. Neteru (plural of neter/netert) are the divine principles and functions of the One Supreme God.

2. You may find variations in writing the same Ancient Egyptian term, such as Amen/Amon/Amun or Pir/Per. This is because the vowels you see in translated Egyptian texts are only approximations of sounds, which are used by Western Egyptologists to help them pronounce the Ancient Egyptian terms/words.

3. We will be using the most commonly recognized words for the English-speaking people that identify a neter/ netert [god, goddess] or a pharaoh or a city; followed by other 'variations' of such a word/term.

It should be noted that the real names of the deities (gods, goddesses) were kept secret so as to guard the cosmic power of the deity. The Neteru were referred to by epithets that describe a particular quality, attribute, and/or aspect(s) of their roles. Such applies to all common terms such as Isis, Osiris, Amun, Re, Horus, etc.

4. When using the Latin calendar, we will use the following terms:

BCE – Before Common Era. Also noted in other references as BC.

CE – Common Era. Also noted in other references as AD.

5. The term Baladi will be used throughout this book to denote the present silent majority of Egyptians that adhere to the Ancient Egyptian traditions, with a thin exterior layer of Islam.[See *Ancient Egyptian Culture Revealed,* by Moustafa Gadalla, for detailed information.]

6. There were/are no Ancient Egyptian writings/texts that were categorized by the Egyptians themselves as "religious", "funerary", "sacred", etc. Western academia gave the Ancient Egyptian texts arbitrary names such as the "Book of This" and the "Book of That", "divisions", "utterances", "spells", etc. Western academia even decided that a certain "Book" had a "Theban version" or "this or that time period version". After believing their own inventive creation, academia then accused the Ancient Egyptians of making mistakes and missing portions of their writings (?!!).

For ease of reference, we will mention the common but arbitrary Western academic categorization of Ancient Egyptian texts, even though the Ancient Egyptians themselves never did.

4

THE 28 ABGD LETTERS & PRONUNCIATIONS

– Actual Egyptian 28 ABGD letters are indicated in Capitals. Non-capital letters are inserted to help English-speaking people pronounce the Egyptian words.

– When 2 letters are underlined together (in the "Roman" script), they represent one sound. For example: Th sounds like the 'Th' in the English word 'Three'. Another example is: Dh sounds like the 'Th' in the English word 'There'.

– An underlined letter followed by a dot indicates an Egyptian letter close to the English sound of such a letter.

– Three Egyptian letters [A, W & Y] are "weak consonants" i.e. each can be pronounced as either a consonant or a vowel sound, depending on the word and its context.

Letter Sound	Numerical Value	Letter sound in English words
1. **ALeF**	1	**A**dam (as a cons.), f**a**t (as a vowel sound)
2. **BeYT**	2	**B**oy
3. **GyM**	3	**G**irl
4. **DaL**	4	**D**elta
5. **Heh**	5	**H**e
6. **Waw**	6	**W**e (as a cons. sound), F**OO**D (as a vowel sound)
7. **Zayn**	7	**Z**ero
8. **H.et**	8	strongly aspirant H made in the throat and is defined as a 'fricative faucal,' that is a strongly marked continuous guttural sound produced at the back of the palate. The sound does not exist in English, French, or Italian, but comes near to the ch in the German lachen, or the Scotch loch (Spanish x and j.)
9. **T.a**	9	emphatic T (close to the sound of double 't' at the end of the English word 'butt')
10. **Yad**	10	**Y**es (as a cons. sound), F**ee**t (as a vowel sound), a semi-consonantal glide, like the y in "yellow"
11. **Kaf**	20	Mil**k**
12. **Lam**	30	**L**ane
13. **Meem**	40	**M**ilk
14. **Noon**	50	**N**o
15. **Seen**	60	**S**afe
16. **A.yn**	70	does not occur in English, but represents a deeper guttural consonant, perhaps a voiced glottal stop
17. **F**	80	**F**ood

No.	Value	Description
18. **S.ad**	90	emphatic S (close to the sound of letter 's' in the English word 'sun' or in the name 'Sandra')
19. **Qaf**	100	It is defined as a 'hard explosive ultra guttural,' and may be described as a guttural having an affinity with k, but formed further back, between the posterior soft portion of the palate and the back of the tongue. Sounds like a backward k; rather like q in queen
20. **R**	200	**R**ise
21. **Sheen**	300	**Sh**ow
22. **T**	400	**T**able
23. **Th**	500	**Th**ree
24. **Kh**	600	Gutteral Aspirate—like ch in Schotch loch—perhaps like ch in German ich
25. **Dhal**	700	O**Th**er
26. **D.ad**	800	emphatic D
27. **Z.**	900	emphatic Z
28. **Ghyn**	1000	A voiced velar fricative /ɣ/ or a voiced uvular fricative

5

MAP OF ANCIENT EGYPT

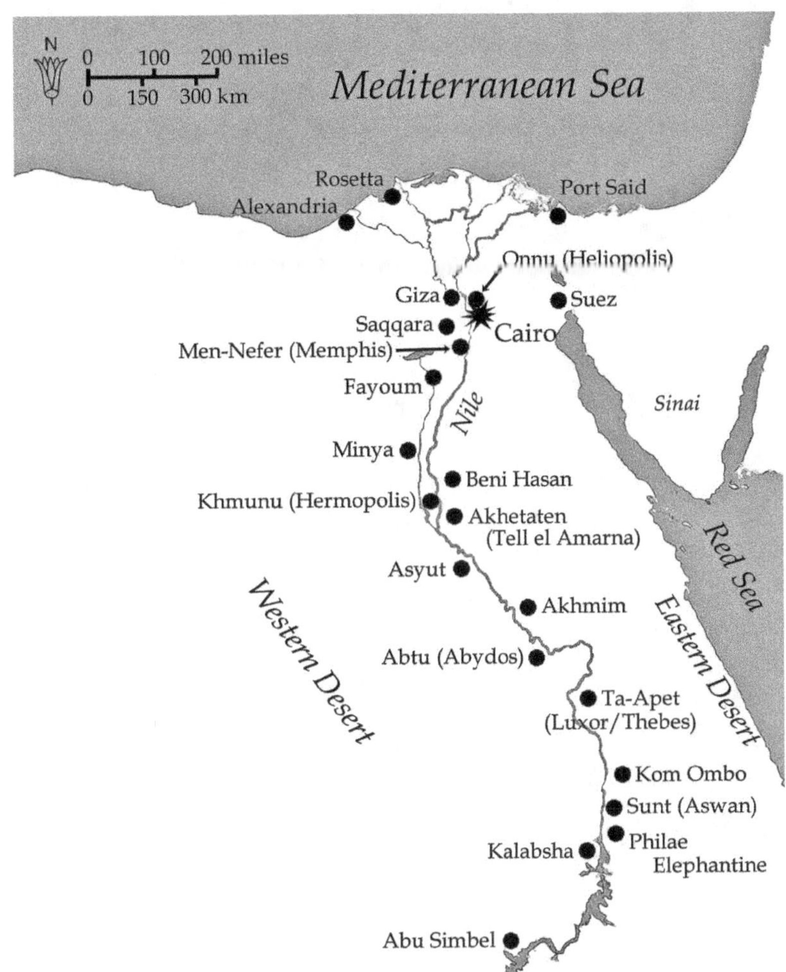

N
0   100   200 miles
0   150   300 km
Mediterranean Sea
Rosetta
Alexandria
Port Said
Onnu (Heliopolis)
Giza
Suez
Saqqara
Cairo
Men-Nefer (Memphis)
Fayoum
Nile
Sinai
Minya
Beni Hasan
Khmunu (Hermopolis)
Akhetaten
(Tell el Amarna)
Asyut
Red Sea
Akhmim
Western Desert
Abtu (Abydos)
Eastern Desert
Ta-Apet
(Luxor/Thebes)
Kom Ombo
Sunt (Aswan)
Kalabsha
Philae
Elephantine
Abu Simbel

PART I : EGYPTIAN ALPHABETICAL LETTERS OF CREATION CYCLE

Chapter 1 : Historical Deception of the (Ancient) Egyptian Linguistics

1.1 THE HIEROGLYPHICS SMOKE SCREEN

The BIGGEST smoke screen in history is concealing the (ancient) Egyptian alphabetical writing system. Western Egyptologists made everyone think of the Egyptian language as a collection of "primitive pictures" called Hieroglyphics. They concealed the Egyptian alphabetical system as the MOTHER of ALL languages in the world.

Here is how Alan Gardiner in his book *Egyptian Grammar* tried to "rationalize" how they concealed the Egyptian alphabetical system. In his book *Egyptian Grammar*, Gardiner writes:

> *"Egyptologists have experienced the practical need of adopting some common standard to which different hieratic hands could be reduced, and instead of selecting one simple style of hieratic for the purpose, have preferred to transcribe all hieratic hands into hieroglyphic".*

Gardiner's "explanation/justification" for burying alphabetical [hieratic] writings assures that there were <u>various forms of writings for various purposes</u>. The very same Western academies NEVER used the same "lame excuse" with Greek, Roman, or any other language in the world.

This lame excuse was ONLY used in Egyptian writings to deceive and conceal the Ancient Egyptian alphabetical writing language.

There is NOT A SINGLE reference prior to this 19th-20th century "Western Egyptologist" conspiracy that stated a relationship between Hieroglyphics (pictorial signs) and Hieratic/demotic (alphabetical signs). On the contrary, EVERY single reference stated, EXPLICITLY, how unrelated they are.

1.2 THE (ANCIENT) EGYPTIAN ALPHABETICAL FORM OF WRITING

The most eminent authority on languages, Isaac Taylor, in his book *History of the Alphabets,* Volume 1, page 62, says:

> *"The immensely early date at which <u>symbols of an alphabetic nature are found on the Egyptian monuments is a fact of great interest</u> and importance. It is of great interest, inasmuch as it constitutes the starting point in the history of the Alphabet, establishing <u>the literal truth of the assertion that the letters of the alphabet are older than the pyramids—older probably than any other existing monument of human civilization</u>".*

Isaac Taylor in his book *History of the Alphabets* Volume I, page 64, wrote about the Egyptian King Sent:

> *"King Sent, in whose reign the alphabetic characters were already in use, may be taken to have lived between 4000 and 4700 BCE. Startling as the result of such calculations may appear, it must be affirmed to be probable that the beginnings of the graphic art <u>in the valley of the Nile must be relegated to a date of seven or eight thousand years from the present time</u>."*

It is very clear that the Ancient Egyptian alphabetical language was the FIRST in the world thousands of years prior to the much ado-about nothing "Sinai scripts".

The more one studies the various languages (and dialects) of the world, the more it becomes clearer and clearer that there was originally one language that split into various tongues. The Bible and ancient writers confirm such an original language. Because of false pride and the prejudices of Western academia and religious (Judaism, Christianity, and Islam) zealots, the origin of this universal mother language has been ignored.

Evidence confirms that Ancient Egypt is the single source of the universal language. On this subject matter, Plato admits the role of Egypt in his Collected Dialogues [Philebus 18-b, c, d]. For now, we shall only refer to the recognition of the Egyptian alphabetic letters indicative of the unity of speech and script. In Philebus [18-d]:

> *"..he [the Ancient Egyptian Theuth (Thoth)] conceived of 'letter' as a kind of bond of unity, uniting as it were all these sounds into one, and so he gave utterance to the expression <u>'art of letters,' implying that there was one art that dealt with the sounds</u>."*

It is very clear that Plato (in Philebus [18-b, c, d]) did not refer to pictorial forms of expression (hieroglyphs), but rather to expression by individual and diverse letters, each with its particular sound value. Other classical writers also stated that Egypt was the original source of alphabets.

Most modern Western scholars affirm explicitly and implicitly that the Ancient Egyptian alphabet (and language) is the oldest source in the world. In his book, *The Literature of the Ancient Egyptians* [page xxxiv-v], the German Egyptologist Adolf Erman admits:

> *"The Egyptians alone were destined to adopt a remarkable method, following which they attained to the highest form of writing, the alphabet. . ."*

The British Egyptologist, W.M. Flinders Petrie, in his book *The Formation of the Alphabets* [page 3], concluded:

"From the beginning of the prehistoric ages, a cursive system consisting of linear signs, full of variety and distinction was certainly used in Egypt."

Petrie has collected and tabulated alphabetical letterforms from very different ages; the earliest belong to the early prehistoric age of Egypt, probably before 7000 BCE, extending to the Greek and Roman Eras. Petrie also compiled (from several independent sources) similar-looking alphabetical letterforms from 25 locations in Asia Minor, Greece, Italy, Spain, and other locations throughout Europe.

Petrie's tabulation of these alphabetical letter-forms shows that:

1. All alphabetical letter-forms were present in Ancient Egypt since early pre-dynastic eras (over 7,000 years ago) prior to anyplace else in the world.

2. All the Egyptian alphabetical letter-forms are clearly distinguishable in the oldest recovered so-called Egyptian "hieratic writing" more than 5,000 years ago.

3. The same exact Ancient Egyptian letter-forms were later adopted and spread by other people throughout the world.

The Ancient Egyptian texts reflect the high culture of the Egyptian language and people. The German Egyptologist Adolf Erman, in his book *The Literature of the Ancient Egyptians* [page xxiv], wrote:

"As far back as we can trace it, the Egyptian language displays signs of being carefully fostered. It is rich in metaphors and figures of speech, a "cultured language", which "composes and thinks" for the person who writes."

The British Egyptologist Alan Gardiner, in his book *Egyptian Grammar* [page 4], wrote:

"No less salient a characteristic of the language is its concision; the phrases and sentences are brief and to the point. Involved constructions and lengthy periods are rare, though such are found in some legal documents. The vocabulary was very rich. The clarity of Egyptian is much aided by a strict word-order. . ."

"For pithiness of proverbs, oracles and sentences, no language can parallel with it.

In axioms, maxims and aphorisms, it is excellent above all other languages.

For definitions, divisions and distinctions, no language is so apt."

1.3 EGYPTIAN IS DEAD—LONG LIVE "ARABIC"!

It has been stated and repeated that the Ancient Egyptian vocalic linguistic system died and was replaced by a brand new language called "Arabic". Nothing can be further from the truth. Alan Gardiner in his book *Egyptian Grammar*, page 3, stated:

"The entire vocalic system of Old Egyptian may indeed be proved to have reached a stage resembling that of Hebrew or modern Arabic"

To say that Egyptians speak "Arabic" is totally false and illogical. It is the other way around—the "Arabs" have long ago "adopted" and continue to speak EGYPTIAN.

A much detailed analysis of this and other languages in the world as they relate to the Ancient Egyptian archetypal vocalic and alphabetical writing system can be found in *The Ancient Egyptian Universal Writing Modes* by Moustafa Gadalla.

1.4 THE REAL AND "FABRICATED" SEQUENCE OF THE ALPHABETS

Western Egyptologists contrary to ALL historical evidence declared that they "settled" on an arbitrary selection of 24 letters to be the Egyptian Alphabet!!!

To further conceal the TRUTH, they arbitrarily arranged their 24 letters based on "frequency of use in texts". They have never applied the same "methodology" to "Greek", "Latin" or any other language!

Some contrary evidence was mistakenly left among these conspirators. A well known reference "Atlas of Ancient Egypt" admits Egyptians had an orderly sequence of alphabet letters. Buried on page 198 of this reference we read:

> ***The Egyptians dissolved their language into a syllabary and had an <u>"alphabetical order into which lists were sometimes arranged"</u>***

The fact of the matter is that the order of the Ancient Egyptian alphabet was the ABGD sequence. The Hebrews followed/follow this sequence and the Arabs, only in the 10th Century, changed the ABGD sequence through a childish reshuffling of the ABGD sequence. (More details can be found in *The Ancient Egyptian Universal Writing Modes* by Moustafa Gadalla.)

It should also be noted that in the early history of modern Egyptology, two centuries ago, scholars followed the ABGD sequence while working on Egyptian monuments such as the work done on Rosetta Stone. Later on, they ignored it for their haphazardly-created sequence! It was an intentional confusion so that nobody would notice the obvious: that Ancient Egyptian letterforms are the archetypal of letterforms for all other languages.

1.5 EGYPTIAN COSMOLOGY AND ALLEGORIES

As a result of the present-day assembly line "education" system, many are incapable of understanding the Ancient Egyptian texts and thoughts. To overcome such mental obstacles, it is therefore important to recognize the Ancient Egyptian mode of expression in the various subjects of their culture—such as religion.

The cosmological knowledge of Ancient Egypt was expressed in story form, which is a superior means for expressing both physical and metaphysical concepts. Well crafted allegories are the only way to explain the deepest truths about God, creation, life, the soul, our place in the universe, and our struggle to evolve to higher levels of insight and understanding.

Allegories are an intentionally chosen means for communicating knowledge. Allegories dramatize cosmic laws, principles, processes, relationships and functions, and express them in an easy to understand way. Once the inner meanings of the allegories have been revealed, they become marvels of simultaneous scientific and philosophical completeness and conciseness. The more they are studied, the richer they become. The 'inner dimension' of the teachings embedded into each story are capable of revealing several layers of knowledge, according to the stage of development of the listener. The "secrets" are revealed as one evolves higher. The higher we get, the more we see. It is always there.

Any good writer or lecturer knows that stories are the best means for explaining the behavior of things because the relationships of parts to each other, and to the whole, are better maintained by the mind. The Egyptian sages transformed common factual nouns and adjectives (indicators of qualities) into proper but conceptual nouns. These were, in addition, personified so that they could be woven into narratives.

The Egyptians did not believe their allegories to be historical facts. They believed IN them, in the sense that they believed in the truth behind the stories.

The Ancient Egyptians had numerous allegories, such as the Isis/Osiris/Horus allegory.

The foremost author of the European Renaissance, namely Athanasius Kircher, wrote in his book *Oedipus Aegyptiacus* (Vol. II, i, p. 40):

> *"The wisdom of the Egyptians was nothing other than this: to represent the science of Divinity and Nature under various fables and allegorical tales of animals and other natural things"*

Chapter 2 : The Principles and Principals of Creation

2.1 THE EGYPTIAN CREATION ACCOUNTS—OVERVIEW

The origin of the world and the nature of the neteru [gods, goddesses] who took part in its creation were subjects of constant interest to the Egyptians.

Ancient Egyptians had four main cosmological teaching centers at Heliopolis, Memphis, Thebes, and Hermopolis (Khmunu). Each center revealed one of the principle phases or aspects of genesis.

Of most interest to us in the subject of this book is the fourth cosmological center at Hermopolis (Khmunu) that provided an account of creation as a result of the Word-analogous to the opening of the Gospel according to St. John.

2.2 IN THE BEGINNING

Every Egyptian creation text begins with the same basic belief that before the beginning of things, there was a liquidy primeval abyss—everywhere, endless, and without boundaries or directions. Egyptians called this cosmic ocean/watery chaos Nu/Ny/Nun—the un-polarized state of matter.

Scientists agree with the Ancient Egyptian description of the origin of the universe as being an abyss. Scientists refer to this abyss as neutron soup, where there are neither electrons nor protons; only neutrons forming one huge, extremely dense nucleus.

Such chaos, in the pre-creation state, was caused by the compression of matter. Atoms did not exist in their normal states, but were squeezed so closely together that many atomic nuclei were crowded into a space previously occupied by a single normal atom. Under such conditions, the electrons of these atoms were squeezed out of their orbits and moved about freely in a chaotic degenerate state.

Nu/Ny/Nun is the "Subjective Being", the symbol of the unformed, undefined, undifferentiated energy/matter, inert or inactive; the uncreated state before the creation. It cannot be the cause of its transformation.

The deeply religious Egyptians, recognizing that no human being can define the undefinable, believed in the presence of an unlimited, unknowable power that is too majestic to communicate with the created universe – but without this power, no creation can exist.

Outside the universe and its cyclical nature is what the Ancient Egyptians referred to as Amen-Renef, which is not the name of any entity, but a sentence that means *That with Unknown Essence*. In this realm of the unknowable, no words in terms of any human thought could be spoken -(and the deeply religious Egyptians never did): and they could only be conveyed by negation of all qualities. The Egyptians would say:

> ***"Whose name is unknown to all neteru***
>
> ***Who has no definition,*** [i.e. cannot be defined/described in any human term.]
>
> ***Who has no image.***
>
> ***Who has no form.***
>
> ***Who has no beginning and no end"***; etc., etc.

As such, the Ancient Egyptian expression Amen-Renef transcends even the quality of being. Amen-Renef is not the Creator or the First-Cause. All the terms God, Creator, Master of the Universe, First Cause, The First are lower principles and are separate from Amen-Renef.

The Egyptians uttered no more of it—and then under infinite reserve, appealing always to a deep sense behind the words—that Amen-Renef is everywhere in the sense that without its Supra-Existence nothing could be.

Now acknowledging Amen-Renef, whose essence is unknown, we can enter the realms of the creation cycles, of which we are a part.

2.3 THE ENERGIES OF THE CREATION CYCLE

The condensed energy in the pre-creation neutron soup was continuously building up. This condensed energy reached the optimum concentration of buildup energy that led to its explosion and expansion outwardly, about 15 billion years ago. The loud sound of this explosion is what caused the break-up of the constituent parts of the universe.

The Ancient Egyptian texts likewise repeatedly stressed that the divine commanding voice/sound was the cause of creation.

The earliest recovered Ancient Egyptian texts 5,000 years ago shows the belief that the Word caused the creation of the World. The Egyptian *Book of the Coming Forth by Light* (wrongly and commonly translated as the *Book of the Dead*), the oldest written text in the world, states:

> *"I am the Eternal ... I am that which created the Word ... I am the Word ..."*

We also find in the *Book of the Divine Cow* (found in the shrines of Tut-Ankh-Amen) that the heavens and its hosts came into existence merely by pronouncing words whose sound alone evokes things. As its name is pronounced, so the thing comes into being.

For the name is a reality the thing itself. In other words, each particular sound has/is its corresponding form. Modern science has confirmed a direct relationship between sound wave frequency and form.

The word (any word) is scientifically a vibrational complex element, which is a wave phenomenon characterized by movement of variable frequency and intensity. In other words, sound is caused by compressing air particles—by rearranging the spacing and movement of air particles, i.e. creating forms. Each sound wave frequency has its own geometrical corresponding form.

The divine sound transformed the potential inert energy/matter in Nun into the parts of the universe as differentiated, orderly, structured kinetic energies in the form of objects, thoughts, forces, physical phenomena, etc.

Transforming one type of energy (potential) into another type (kinetic) made the universe come to life, in whole and in its constituent parts.

It is all a matter of energies.

So, let us go back to our main topic, which is the creation cycle.

Creation came out of the state of no-creation. The Egyptians called it Nun. None or nil also represents the pre-creation state of the universe. There is NO universe: NONE NILL ZERO. Such a state of the universe represents the Subjective Being—unformed, undefined, and undifferentiated energy/matter. Its inert energy is inactive.

On the other hand, the creation state is orderly, formed, defined, and differentiated. The totality of the divine energy during the creation state is called Atam by the Egyptians.

Atam means *the One-ness of all, the complete*. It is connected with the root, 'tam' or 'tamam', meaning *"to be complete"* or *"to make an end of"*.

In Ancient Egyptian texts Atam means *he who completes or perfects,* and in the Litany of Re, Atam is recognized as *the Complete One, the ALL*.

The Ancient Egyptian texts emphasize that the complete one contains all. The Ancient Egyptian text reads:

> *"I am many of names and many of forms, and my Being exists in every neter".*

Numerically, one is not a number, but the essence of the underlying principle of number,- all other numbers being made of it. One represents Unity: the Absolute as un-polarized energy. Atam as the number One is neither odd nor even but both. Atam is neither female nor male, but both.

Atam is the totality of the orderly energy matrix during the creation stage, while Nun is the disorderly energy compound—the Subjective Being. The total divine energy within the universe is called Nun in its chaotic state and Atam in its orderly creation and its point of state/process.

Atam represents the release, in an orderly sequence, of the existing energy within Nun, i.e. bringing it to life. This represents the Objective Being.

The seed of creation out of which everything originated is Atam. And just as the plant is contained within the seed, so everything that is created in the universe is Atam, too.

* Atam, the One who is the All, as the Master of the Universe,

declares, in the Ancient Egyptian papyrus commonly known as the *Bremner-Rhind Papyrus*:

> ***"When I manifested myself into existence, existence existed.***
>
> ***I came into existence in the form of the Existent, which came into existence in the First Time.***
>
> ***Coming into existence according to the mode of existence of the Existent, I therefore existed.***
>
> ***And it was thus that the Existent came into existence".***

In other words, when the Master of the Universe came into existence, the whole creation came into existence, because the Complete One contains the all.

The Ancient Egyptian texts emphasize that the complete one contains all. The Ancient Egyptian text reads:

> ***"I am many of names and many of forms, and my Being exists in every neter".***

The cycle of creation is caused and maintained by divine forces or energies. These energies like the perpetual cycle of creation go through a process of transformation from birth-life-aging-dying-death to rebirth. We, as human beings, have similar life forces that change throughout our lifetime. Our human bodies consist of numerous cycles that govern our life existence. All forces die out when we die.

The Egyptians called these divine forces neteru. The main theme of the universe is its cyclical nature. The NeTeRu are the forces of NaTuRe which make the world go around so to speak. To simply call them gods and goddesses gives a false impression.

The Divine energy that manifests itself in the creation cycle is defined by its constituent energy aspects that were called neteru by the Ancient Egyptians. In order for creation to exist and to be maintained, this divine energy must be thought of in terms of male and female principles. Therefore, Ancient Egyptians expressed the cosmic energy forces in the terms of netert (female principle) and neter (male principle).

The Egyptian word neter or nature or netjer means a power that is able to generate life and to maintain it when generated. As all parts of creation go through the cycle of birth-life-death-rebirth, so do the driving energies during the stages of this cycle. It is therefore that the Ancient Egyptian neteru being divine energies went and continue to go through the same cycle of birth-growth-death and renewal. Such understanding was common to all, as noted by Plutarch, that the multitude forces of nature known as neteru are born or created, are subject to continuous changes, age and die and are reborn.

We can give the example of the caterpillar that is born, lives, then builds its own cocoon, where it dies or better yet transforms into a butterfly who lays eggs, and on and on. What we have here is the cyclical transformation from one form/state of energy to another.

Another example is the water cycle—the water that evaporates, forming clouds that rain back to earth. It is all an orderly cyclical transformation of energies in various forms.

When you think of neteru not as gods and goddesses but the cosmic energy forces, one can see the Ancient Egyptian system as a brilliant representation of the universe. Philosophically, this cyclical natural transformation is applicable to our saying

"The more things change, the more they stay the same".

In scientific circles, this is known as the **natural law of conservation of energy**, which is described as: *the principle that energy is never consumed but only changes form, and that the total energy in* *a physical system, such as the universe, cannot be increased or diminished.*

This matrix of energies came as a result of the initial act of creation and the subsequent effects of the Big Bang that created the universe. This matrix consists of an organized hierarchy. Each level of the hierarchy of existence is a theophany—a creation by the consciousness of the level of being above it. The self-contemplation by each stage of existence brings into being each lower stage. As such, the hierarchy of energies is interrelated, and each level is sustained by the level below it. This hierarchy of energies is set neatly into a vast matrix of deeply interfaced natural laws. It is both physical and metaphysical.

The Ancient and Baladi Egyptians made/make no distinction between a metaphysical state of being and one with a material body. Such a distinction is a mental illusion. We exist on a number of different levels at once, from the most physical to the most metaphysical. Einstein agreed with the same principles.

Since **Einstein's relativity theory**, it has been known and accepted that matter is a form of energy a coagulation or condensation of energy. As a result, the natural law for the conservation of matter or mass similarly states that matter is neither created nor destroyed during any physical or chemical change.

Energy is made up of molecules rotating or vibrating at various rates of speed. In the "physical" world, molecules rotate at a very slow and constant rate of speed. That is why things appear to be solid to our earthly senses. The slower the speed, the more dense or solid the thing. In the metaphysical (spirit) world, the molecules vibrate at a much faster or ethereal dimension where things are freer and less dense.

In this light, the universe is basically a hierarchy of energies at different orders of density. Our senses have some access to the densest form of energy, which is matter. The **hierarchy of ener-**

gies is interrelated, and each level is sustained by the level below it. This hierarchy of energies is set neatly into a vast matrix of deeply interfaced natural laws. It is both physical and metaphysical.

The universal energy matrix encompasses the world as a product of a complex system of relationships among people (living and dead), animals, plants, and natural and supernatural phenomena. This rationale is often called Animism because of its central premise that all things are animated (energized) by life forces. Each minute particle of everything is in constant motion, i.e. energized, as acknowledged in kinetic theory. In other words, everything is animated (energized)—animals, trees, rocks, birds even the air, sun, and moon.

The created universe was caused by the expulsion forces, which cause all galaxies to move outwardly. Such expulsion forces are being opposed by the gravitational/contractional forces, which pull the galaxies together. At the present time, the outwardly forces exceed the contractional forces and therefore the limits of the universe are still expanding.

Scientists tell us that at a certain point in time in the future, the universe will stop expanding and will start getting smaller. The microwave radiation from the Big Bang fireball (which is still rushing around) will start squashing down and will heat up and change color again, until it becomes visible once more. The sky will become red, and will then turn orange, yellow, white, and will end in the Big Crunch when all the matter and all the radiation in the universe will come crashing together, into one unit.

The Big Crunch is not the end by itself for the reunited crunched universe—neutron soup—will have the potential for a new creation, which is called the Big Bounce.

So it is not surprising that the Ancient Egyptian texts did also describe, in the usual Egyptian symbolic terms The Big Crunch and the Big Bounce.

The Egyptian coffin texts, Spell 130, tells us that

> ***"After the millions of years of differentiated creation the chaos before creation will return. Only the Complete One [Atam] and Aus-Ra will remain no longer separated in space and time".***

The Ancient Egyptian text tells us two points. The first is the return of the created universe to chaos at the end of the creation cycle, which signifies the Big Crunch. The second point is the potential for a new cyclical rebirth of the universe as symbolized by the presence of **Aus-Ra** [commonly known as Osiris; representing the cyclical aspect of creation].

The system of creation is a system of necessary emanation, procession, or irradiation accompanied by necessary aspiration or reversion-to-source where all the forms and phases of Existence flow from the Divinity and all strive to return thither and to remain there.

Chapter 3 : The Cosmic Manifestation of the Egyptian Alphabet

3.1 THE FORMATIVE LOGOS (SOUND AND FORM)

Our focus here in this book is on the aspect of the creation process that comes as a result of the Divine Word.

Egyptian creation texts repeatedly stress the belief of creation by the Word. When nothing existed except the One, he created the universe with his commanding voice. The Egyptian *Book of the Coming Forth by Light* (wrongly and commonly translated as the *Book of the Dead*), the oldest written text in the world, states:

> *I am the Eternal ... I am that which created the Word ... I am the Word ...*

In Ancient Egypt, the words of Re, revealed through Thoth (Tehuti), became the things and creatures of this world, i.e. the words (meaning sound waves) created the forms in the universe.

The word (any word) is scientifically a vibrational complex element which is a wave phenomenon characterized by movement of variable frequency and intensity. In other words, sound is caused by compressing air particles—by rearranging the spacing and movement of air particles, creating forms. Each sound wave frequency has its own geometrical corresponding form.

Egyptian creation texts repeatedly stress the belief of creation by the Word. We find that in the *Book of the Divine Cow* (found in the shrines of Tut-Ankh- Amen), Re creates the heavens and its hosts merely by pronouncing some words whose sound alone evokes the names of things, and these things then appear at his bidding. As its name is pronounced, so the thing comes into being. For the name is a reality; the thing itself. In other words, each particular sound has/is its corresponding form, as stated earlier in this chapter.

The role of the name in Ancient and Baladi Egypt was not, as per our modern-day thinking, a mere label. The name of a neter, person, animal, or principle represents a resume or synopsis of the qualities of that person or object. To know and pronounce the real name of a neter (god), man, or animal is to exercise power over it. It is thus that Ancient and Baladi Egyptians have real "secret" names for everybody and everything, in order to protect the person and the thing.

Creation is therefore a relation of identity; a complete congruence between 'image' and 'object;' between the name and the thing.

3.2 THE COSMIC FORMATION OF ALPHABETS

Thoth (Tehuti) represents the Divine Messenger who articulates and writes the spoken/written language, knowledge, etc.

Thoth (Tehuti) is portrayed as an ibis-headed figure, writing on a tablet.

Several of Thoth's attributes were confirmed by Diodorus of Sicily, in his *Book I*, Section 16-1:

> *"It was by Thoth, according to Ancient Egyptians, that <u>the common language of mankind was first further articulated</u>, and that many objects which were still nameless received an appellation, that <u>the alphabet were defined</u>,"*

The Ancient Egyptians considered the letters to be elemental, basic things in a very real sense. For the Stoics, it appears that language was not simply modeled after the physical world, but belonged to it part and parcel. It was customary among the Egyptians to identify the letters of the alphabet (and with them, the individual sounds of speech) as stoicheia – literally, physical particles. Throughout the history, the alphabet was invested with very real mundane significance. To these Egyptians, letters are things, not pictures of things.

Plato's Collected Dialogues refers to the Ancient Egyptian writing mode in *Philebus* [18-b, c, d]

> *"...he [Theuth/Thoth] found a number of the things, and affixed to the whole collection, as to each single member of it, the name 'letter.' ... he [Theuth/Thoth] conceived of 'letter' as a kind of bond of unity, uniting as it were all these sounds into one, and so he gave utterance to the expression 'art of letters,' implying that there was one art that dealt with the sounds."*

The Ancient Egyptian alphabet consists of 28 letters [25 consonants and 3 primary vowels]. Plutarch referred to such a fact in his *Moralia Volume V*, [56A],

> ***"Five makes a square of itself, as many as the letters of the Egyptian alphabet."***

The three primary vowels A, Y and W were not counted in the number of the 25 consonants/letters because they were/are not produced by the articulating organs. Such practice was universal at that time. Moreover, it continues to be endorsed by modern day linguists and philologists.

The whole alphabet, read in its proper order, is a natural symbol of Creation. It represents through the letters the necessary basic processes and structural requirements common to any creation or making, including that of the universe, so far as is humanly discernible.

The great chain joining the upper world with the lower knows all the mysteries of nature, and becomes a worker of miracles.

3.3 THE LUNAR MANIFESTATIONS OF THE ALPHABETICAL LETTERS

Thoth (Tehuti) , the Divine Messenger is not a neter (god) of the moon, but a moon-neter. There is a subtle difference between these two concepts which must be borne in mind in order to understand the character and significance of Thoth. Thoth manifests himself in and through the moon. This celestial body is the nature-substratum of his being.

The relation of the power of speech to that of the intellect is like that of the moon to the sun. The moon derives its light from the sun in the course of traversing twenty-eight mansions of the moon. In the same way the faculty of speech derives the meaning of the words from the intellect in the course of traversing the throat and interpreting it through the medium of the twenty-eight letters of the [Egyptian] alphabet. The relation of the twenty-eight letters of the alphabet to the power of speech is like the relation of the twenty-eight mansions to the moon.

The moon, being the planet closest to the Earth, acts as the intermediary between all the heavens and the terrestrial domain so that the lunar mansions synthesize in themselves all the aspects of the Intellect which are manifested in the planetary spheres and the archetypal world of signs. The numerical symbolism involved clarifies this relation. The number of the mansions of the Moon, which is 28, is equal to $7 + 6 + 5 + 4 + 3 + 2 + 1$ that is, the sum of the number of planets. Moreover, the 28 mansions are the macrocosmic counterparts of the 28 letters of the Egyptian alphabet which form the language of the Divine Word.

3.4 THE SEQUENCE OF THE CREATION CYCLE

Creation is the sorting out (giving definition to/bringing order to) of all the chaos (the undifferentiated energy/matter and consciousness) of the primeval state. All of the Ancient Egyptian accounts of creation are exhibited with orderly, well defined, clearly demarcated stages.

We have seen how an orderly creation in the form of Atam, the Complete One emerged out of the pre-creation chaotic state of the Nun—the nothingness.

Throughout the Ancient Egyptian texts, we consistently find how one state of being develops or better yet emerges into the next state of being. And we always find that any two consecutive states are images of each other. Not only is that scientifically correct; but it is orderly, natural, and poetic. The Egyptians were famous for writing these scientific and philosophical subjects in poetic forms.

Just like the sequence of creation **as** it unfolds, each stage contains all subsequent stages.

The first letter 'A' was associated with all the other letters and all the other letters were associated with 'A'. The second letter 'B' was associated with all the other letters and all the other letters were associated with 'B'. And on and on…

3.5 THOTH AND SESHAT—LETTERS AND NUMBERS

While Thoth represents the Divine attribute of the spoken and written words, his female counterpart Seshat is described as The Enumerator, denoting the divine significance of numbers in the Ancient Egyptian traditions.

Numbers conform to the arrangement of natural things; for most natural things were established by the Creator in orders.

Both language (Thoth) and numbers (Seshat) are simply two aspects of a single scheme. Numbers are the underlying basis of letters. For both the Ancient and Baladi Egyptians, letters can be transposed into numbers and number codes to reconstruct the "true" meaning of certain writings. Transposition was extensively used by the Egyptians. Letters and numbers are reservoirs of divine power. Magic squares utilizing letters in a grid in both their phonetic and numerical aspects have been used by many mystics. The letters form meaningful words or formulae, and the sum of their numerical equivalents when combined in prescribed ways is significant. The letters usually add up to the same number vertically, horizontally, or diagonally. Such magic squares were often used as amulets in ancient times and were very important in medieval mystical practices.

The basic axiom of 'The Science of Letters' is the interaction between letters and their 'relation to numerical proportion' which initiates in the reader the activity of constant association.

The concept that the nature and secret of a letter is alive when it is compounded to form words, while words are correspondingly alive within created things, is the basic principle of the science of letters. All created things move in different stages because of the constant renewal of creation and the secret of all created things lies in the word.

Apart from the combination and interaction of the letters, the meaning of the term also operates on more than one level, mediating between the physical and the metaphysical. This is another important practice by Sufis in their methods of communication. The Sufis believe that the 'word' can be an important realm of mediating between the two worlds. Because it operates on several levels, it is referred to as 'The Secret Language', since understanding depends on the degree of the candidate's enlightenment.

Numbers and letters are one and the same. To distinguish between the two manifestations in the Egyptian texts, numbers are shown in upside down positions of their equivalent/ corresponding letters. An easy example for English speakers is the noticeable similarity between the number 7 and the letter Z. The letter Z is the seventh letter in ABGD sequence.

3.6 THE NUMERICAL VALUES OF THE 28 LETTERS OF THE ALPHABET

Each letter had an underlying numeric as well as a phonetic value. The Egyptians used their alphabet letters as numbers. The number values commonly followed the order of the letters of the particular system (incidentally affording scholars further corroboration of the standard order of the letters), going from one through ten, with the next letter equaling 20, then 30 up through 100, with the next being 200, and so on. When the letters were exhausted, new signs or doubled letters were used to represent very large numbers.

There are two ways in which alphabetical characters may be employed as numerals. The letters may either be taken in their alphabetical order or the initial letters of the words denoting the numbers may be similarly employed.

The above alphabetical and corresponding numeration system were clearly utilized in the famous Ancient Egyptian Leiden Papyrus J 350, which confirms that number symbolism had been practiced in Egypt at least since the Old Kingdom (2575–2150 BCE); a copy of which was reproduced during the reign of Ramses II in the 13th century BCE (since on the back of the papyrus there appears a journal dating from the 52nd year of that pharaoh).

The Leiden Papyrus consists of an extended composition, describing the orderly stages of the creation cycle in poetic stanzas. The "stanzas" are actually called Mansions (of the moon) and are numbered 1, 2...10, 20...100, 200...800. Each stanza [MANSION] begins and ends with a word-play on the number that heads it.

The numbered mansions [stanzas] follow their corresponding alphabetical order of the ABGD sequence. Each identifies its creation stage/role in the creation cycle.

For a complete list of the ABGD letters and their corresponding numbers, check the beginning of this book: The 28 ABGD Letters and Pronunciation.

3.7 THE TRILATERAL STEM VERB—GAMETRIA

All Egyptologists who studied the morphology of Ancient Egyptian words since its earliest history such as Alan Gardiner, Sethe, etc. testified that the archetypal building block in the Egyptian language is the stem/root verb that consists of 3 letters.

The root of each word establishes its character, for it is of the same nature, temper, constitution or genius. The root is an independent entity. The character is a dependent entity; a manifestation of its root. It is of like nature or of peculiar constitution attributable to its root. The properties of a character must agree with its word root as a property of that word root and as an offspring expressing it by its noticeable likeness to it. The word speaks. The literate characters give the sound and substance.

As stated above, the basic axiom of 'The Science of Letters' is the interaction between letters and their 'relation to numerical proportion' which initiates in the reader the activity of constant association.

The concept that the nature and secret of a letter is alive when it is compounded to form words, while words are correspondingly alive within created things, is the basic principle of the science of letters.

All created things move in different stages because of the constant renewal of creation; and the secret of all created things lies in the word.

The intimacy between letters and their equivalent numerical values is also extended into the word formation of letters as extended to the stem verb of any (Egyptian) word. This concept is known as gematria.

In gematrial calculations, the number values are used to reveal inner meanings, correspondences, and associations.

There are different systems for identifying the numerical equivalence of individual letters and how these letters can be calculated according to the implicit word-value of their names. The simplest four ways to calculate the equivalent numerical values are:

1. **Absolute value**—also known as Normative value. Each letter is given the value of its accepted numerical equivalent.

2. **Ordinal value**—each of the 28 letters is given an equivalent from one to 28. For example, 'A' equals 1, 'K' equals 11,'T' = 22.

3. **Reduced value**—based on modulus 9 in mathematical terminology. Each letter is reduced to a figure of one digit. For example, in this reckoning, 'A' equals 1, 'Y' equals 10, Q equals 100 would all have a numerical value of 1; 'B' equals 2, 'K' equals 20, and 'R' equals 200 would all have a numerical value of 2, and so on. Thus, the letters have only nine equivalents.

4. **Integral Reduced**—Here, the total numerical value of a word is reduced to one digit. Should the sum of these numbers exceed 9, the integer values of the total are repeatedly added to each other to produce a single-digit figure. The same value will be arrived at regardless of whether it is the absolute values, the ordinal values, or the reduced values that are being counted.

In the above four simple ways, the weight of the location of each letter in a word has not been accounted for, even though this will be the accurate way to figure out the numerical sum value for a word. In any event, we shall be using the integral reduced method to get the feel of Egyptian words in the rest of this book.

We are going to refer here to one example which is familiar to most people in the world. The number 666 is known as the "devil's number". This can only make sense in the Egyptian alphabetical ABGD system, where:

666 = 6 + 60 + 600

 6 is the numerical value of letter 'W'

 60 is the numerical value of letter 'S'

 600 is the numerical value of letter '<u>Kh</u>'

The word for the number 666 is 'W' 'S' '<u>Kh</u>'. This Egyptian word means 'dirty'/'rotten'/… all the negative attributes of the "devil".

Chapter 4 : The Three Primary Phases of the Creation Cycle

4.1 LEIDEN PAPYRUS' THREE TIERS

The Ancient Egyptian hymns of the Leiden Papyrus J 350 shows the correlation between the Ancient Egyptian Alphabet and their corresponding numerical values that follow the various stages of the creation cycle.

The manuscript is divided into a series of numbered "stanzas". Each is entitled "Mansions [of the moon], number xx".

Each stanza speaks of a specific step in the creation process with many words having a specific letter and corresponding number. In poetic form, the creation process is explained with the very special characteristics of each number and its associated letter.

The numbering system of this Egyptian Papyrus by itself is significant. They are numbered in three tiers—1 to 9, and then the powers 10, 20, 30, to 90—and the third tier is numbered in the 100s.

The Papyrus Leiden J 350 originally contained 26 stanzas(songs)/praises/hymns to praise the attributes (qualities) and the actions of the Divine. The numbered 26 stanzas represent the cycle of creation in alphabetical/numerical sequence.

The first 4 ½ of them had been torn away with the first page.

There were no stanzas for the last 2 letters of the alphabet (#27 and 28), for reasons to be explained in the last part of this book.

4.2 THE THREE PRIMARY ENNEADS OF THE CREATION CYCLE

The division into three parts is a dominant feature of any cycle.

Consistent with the theme of three phases of the creation cycle, we find that as far back as at least 5,000 years ago, the "Pyramid Texts" reveals the existence of three companies of neteru (gods, goddesses), and each company consisted of 9 neteru (gods, goddesses).

Throughout the "Pyramid Texts" frequent mention is made of one group, or of 2 or 3 groups, of 9 neteru (gods, goddesses).

The Universal significance of the number Nine is evident as follows:

- A human child is normally conceived, formed and born in nine months.

- Number nine marks the end of gestation and the end of each series of numbers.

- If multiplied by any other number, it always reproduces itself (3 x 9 = 27 and 2 + 7 = 9 or 6 x 9 = 54 and 5 + 4 = 9. And so on).

- Nine marks the transition from one scale (the numbers from 1 to 9) to a higher scale (starting with 10), and so it is the number of initiation which is again similar to the birth of a baby after nine months.

Nine is the number of each phase of the creation cycle. Each phase begets the following phase in 9 terms.

The Egyptian texts speak of three Enneads—each representing a phase in the creation cycle.

The first (Great) Ennead represents the conceptual or divine stage. This is governed by Re.

The second Ennead represents the manifestation stage. This is governed by Osiris.

The third Ennead represents the return to the Source—combining both Re and Osiris.

In the *Book of the Coming Forth By Light* [commonly and wrongly being called *Book of Dead*], both the souls of Osiris and Re meet and are united to form an entity, described so eloquently:

I am His Two Souls in his Twins.

4.3 LITANY OF RE—THREE PHASES OF CREATION CYCLE (RA & AUS-RA & BOTH)

After a brief preface, the Litany opens with seventy-five invocations to the Forms of Ra/Re, followed by a series of prayers and hymns in which the identity of Re and Osiris is constantly stressed.

The perpetual cycle of Ausar [Osiris] and Ra [Re] dominates the Ancient Egyptian texts. The first leg is the manifestation of Ra [Re] in his forms. The second leg is the manifestation of Aus-Ra [Osiris] in his forms. The third and final leg occurs in the netherlands where both join together and resurrect as a new creation.

The relationship between the cycle of death and resurrection is reflected in the "name" of Ausar [Osiris], which consists of two syllables—Aus-Ra.

The first syllable of the name (Aus-Ra) is pronounced Aus or Us, meaning "strength, might, power".

Aus – Ra then means the strength or source of the Ra.

Ra [Re] is the cosmic principle of energy that moves toward death, and Ausar [Osiris] represents the process of rebirth. Thus, the terms of life and death become interchangeable: life means slow dying, anddeath means resurrection to new life. The dead person in death is identified with Ausar, but he will come to life again and will be identified with Ra.

The *Litany of Re* is basically a detailed amplification of a short passage of Chapter 17 of the *Book of the Coming Forth by Light*, describing the merging of Ausar [Osiris] and Ra [Re] into a Twin Soul.

4.4 SUFISM AND ANCIENT EGYPTIAN THREE PHASES CYCLE

Thoth, the Ancient Egyptian neter (god), is recognized by all early (and later) Sufi writers as the ancient model of alchemy, mysticism, and all related subjects.The well known Sufi writer, Idries Shah admits the role of Egypt via Tehuti and Dhu'I-Nun on Sufism and alchemy as follows:

> *". . . alchemical lore came from Egypt direct from the writings of Thoth . . . According to Sufi tradition the lore was transmitted through Dhu'i-Nun the Egyptian, the King or Lord of the Fish, one of the most famous of classical Sufi teachers. [The Sufis, 1964]"*

More about Ancient Egypt being the sole source of Sufism can be found in *Egyptian Mystics: Seekers of The Way*, by Moustafa Gadalla.

It must be noted and emphasized that these Sufi sages (like others in Greece and elsewhere) never claimed themselves to be the source of such knowledge. They usually begin a sentence by "It was said that...".

Ibn Sina likewise (and in accordance to the Ancient Egyptian system of numbering letters in single, tens, and hundreds) provides the same sequence of creation process. The very name of Ibn Sina—meaning the (son) from (the Egyptian Peninsula of) Sinai—indicates his Egyptian origin. Most importantly, the content of all his accredited writings are of Ancient Egyptian origin and can only be explained in Ancient Egyptian context and no other place. All such Sufi writings on this subject can only be traced to one source—Ancient Egypt.

PART II : THE CONCEIVING PHASE/ENNEAD

Chapter 5 : The Theme of the First Phase/Ennead

The Conceiving Phase/Ennead

The theme of the First Phase (1-9 'A'-'T̲.') is the objectification of a circumscribed area of undifferentiated energy/matter wherein the world will be manifested. It consists of the establishment of order and the co-factors of lifeforms as the foundation for the world.

Creation is the sorting out (giving definition to/bringing order to) of all the chaos (the undifferentiated energy/matter and consciousness) of the primeval state. All of the Ancient Egyptian accounts of creation are exhibited with orderly, well defined, clearly demarcated stages.

Meditation on the sequence of the spheres from the top down reveals a gradual progression of qualities from the undifferentiated to the full differentiation of the tenth sphere—being the beginning of the Second phase of the Creation Cycle.

Phase One consists basically of three consecutive groups, each of which consists of 3 stages/letters/numbers. The sequence flow is as follows:

1- 3   The Primary Trinity—['A', 'B' and 'G']

4-6   Establishing and maintaining order—['D', 'H' and 'W']

7-9   Creating Physical entities and Events—['Z','H.' ,'T.']

In the process of reading about each individual step/realm of this phase, the following points should be kept in mind:

1. Atam is the ONE and All one; and the Creation is the multiplication of his names and his forms, and this creation goes on forever.

2. In the Egyptian texts the neteru (gods, goddesses) are not personalities. They represent cosmic energies, as explained earlier. The names and symbols change their meaning, and a neter (god, goddess) at one given moment may symbolize quite another power at the next.

3. All "references" to "The Pharaoh/king" is actually to 'The Divine Man" or the *divinity in man*.

4. References to animals always represent animal symbolism at work—for example references to the baboon and that of the bull are both allusions to regained sexual power and fertility.

Chapter 6 : The 1st Sphere/ Letter 'A'—Alpha: The One and All

6.1 THE ROLE OF LETTER 'A' IN THE CREATION CYCLE

All of the Ancient Egyptian accounts of creation are exhibited with orderly, well defined, clearly demarcated stages. As the sequence of creation unfolds,each stage contains all subsequent stages.

The first letter 'A' was associated with all the other letters and all the other letters were associated with it. The second letter 'B' was associated with all the other letters and all the other letters were associated with the letter 'B'. And the cycle turns, again and again.

Creation is the self-manifestation of the All who, being one, yet assumes different aspects or forms.

Atam represents THE ONE, or First Existent—The Alpha the first and the foremost.

Atam is recognized in the *Litany of Re*, as ***"The ALL"***.

The seed of creation out of which everything originated, is Atam. and just as the plant is contained within the seed, so everything that is created in the universe is Atam, also.

Atam, the on who is ***The All,*** as the master of the universe declares, in the ancient Egyptian papyrus commonly known as the Bremner-Rhind papyrus:

"When I manifested... existence... existed.

I came into existence... in the form of the Existent... which came into existence in the First Time.

Coming into existence... according to the mode of existence of the Existent... I therefore existed.

And it was thus... that the Existent came into existence".

In other words, when the master of the universe came into existence, the whole creation came into existence, because the complete one contains the all. All Ancient Egyptian texts reflect this sophisticated thought that emphasizes a progressive and orderly sequence of creation.

The first stage of the creation cycle was the self-creation of the Supreme Being as creator and Being i.e., the passage from Subjective Being (Nu/Ny/Nun) to Objective Being (Atam).

In the Unas (so-called Pyramid) Texts, there is the following invocation:

Salutation to thee, Atam,

Salutation to thee, he who comes into being by himself!

*Thou art **high in this thy name High Mound**,* [§1587]

We also find that the First Existence is called El-Bari in the Sufi writings of the Egyptian Ibn Sina. The word used in Ibn Sina's text "El-Bari" is literally an Ancient Egyptian word that had the same meanings in later "Arabic" texts—meaning *standing on land/ solid ground—offshore(coast).*

As such, the writings of Ibn Sina (like others before him and after him) can only be explained in Ancient Egyptian terms simply because Ancient Egypt was their only source of such knowledge.

6.2 THE NUMERICAL SIGNIFICANCE OF 'A'

Numerically, one is not a number but the essence of the underlying principle of number; all other numbers being made of it. One represents Unity: the Absolute as unpolarized energy. It was said that the number One is neither odd nor even, but both; because if it's added to an odd number, it makes it even, and vice-versa. So it combined the opposites of odd and even, and all the other opposites in the universe. One contains ALL the numbers and, likewise, Atam the First Existence contains all subsequent creation. Atam therefore represents the first letter Aleph.

6.3 NAMES & MEANINGS OF LETTER 'A'

All names and words related to the letter 'A' are consistent with its role in the creation cycle i.e.:

'Alef' means *head/leader—Alfa/Alpha*.

'A- L ef' means *to go around* (cycle).

'A L Laf' means *to author*.

Chapter 7 : The 2nd Sphere/ Letter 'B'—The Divine Mind/Consciousness

7.1 THE ROLE OF LETTER 'B' IN THE CREATION CYCLE

The first act of creation is to conceive it—both intellectually and physically.

Atam as THE ONE, or First Existent "develops" into The Divine Mind, or First Thinker and Thought.

This Divine Thought is an Intelligence; or rather, is the Universal Intelligence. As the act, offspring, and image of The First, it is a sort of mediation to us of the Unknowable ONE.

This Divine Intelligence is the image of the One. They are distinctively different, but are derived one from the other.

Since consciousness is immaterial, then it cannot be divided or multiplied. Its consciousness that dwells in living things is the one undivided consciousness of the Supreme Being. The appearance as separate and individuated conscious beings can be understood in the analogy of shining a light through different colored windows. The same light will come out on the other side with entirely different qualities as it shines through a yellow glass, a red glass, and so on. Thus the One Consciousness comes out different as it "shines" through men of different make-ups, dogs, horses, roses, worms, etc.

A portion of an Ancient Egyptian papyrus, known as the *Book of Knowing the Creations of Ra and Overcoming Apep (Apophis)*, reads in part:

> *"I conceived in my own heart; there came into being a vast number of forms of divine beings as the forms of offsprings and the forms of their offsprings..."*

The Ideas, or Divine Thoughts, are Real Beings, Intelligences, Powers: they are the eternal Originals, Archetypes, Intellectual Forms of all that exists in the lower spheres.

Atam represents the realization of the total cosmic existence.

In the Egyptian text, Atam states:

> *"I appeared as Re on the eastern horizon of heaven..."*

Another version in this Ancient Egyptian book reads:

> *"I am Atam (the All) when I was alone in the Watery Abyss.*
>
> *I am Re in his manifestations..."*

Re represents the primeval, cosmic, creative force; the manifestation of Atam.

Isis—as the female principle of creation—is closely related to Atam. Isis in the Ancient Egyptian texts is described as:

> *"The Light-giver in heaven with Re".*

Isis is the emanated energy from the Total One. As the female principle in the universe, only she can conceive and deliver the created universe.

In other words Isis is the Image of the cosmic creative impulse recognized by the term Re. Thus, when speaking of Re, the Ancient Egyptian text says:

"Thou art the bodies of Isis".

This implies that Re, the creative energy, appears in the different aspects of the cosmic female principle Isis. As such, Isis is recognized as:

"The female Re".

"The house/daughter of Re".

The Lady of the beginning of time.

The prototype of all beings.

The greatest of the neteru [the divine forces.]

The Queen of all the neteru.

Daughter,in Egyptian, means **BeT**, which is pronounced by non-Egyptians as *'Beth'*.

House, in Egyptian, is spelled as **BeYT**, but is generally pronounced by Egyptians as *'**BaiT**'*.

The intimacy between the "two" words is unmistakable. Most importantly, "both" begins with the second letter of the alphabet, being 'B'.

The second letter 'B' denotes the physical and metaphysical conception of creation—Divine Intelligence as well as the "house" being the Universal Womb/Space/Bubble that will contain the created universe.

It should be noted that Sufi traditions also speak of 'A.QL eL KuL'—Universal Intellect as represented by the second letter 'B'—being the second lunar mansion.

'A.QL eL KuL' means Intelligence (A.QL)—Universal/All (eL KuL)—Universal Intelligence.

Numerically <u>A</u>.QL = 70 + 100 + 30 = 200 →(reduced to) 2—Being Letter '**B**' as well as being Isis' number, as shown later in this chapter.

Isis is the power responsible for the creation of all living creatures. Ancient Egyptians called her Isis with the 10,000 Names/Attributes. Plutarch took note of that and wrote in his *Moralia Vol. V:*

> *"Isis is, in fact, the female principle of Nature, and is <u>receptive of every form of generation</u>, in accord with which she is called by Plato the gentle nurse and the all-receptive, and by most people has been called by countless names, since, because of <u>the force of Reason</u>, she turns herself to this thing or that and is receptive of all manner of shapes and forms."*

In the following chapter we will see how the letter '**B**' will engender the third letter '**G**'. The Supreme Intellectual Principle cannot be unproductive; accompanying its Act of Thought is Act of Act. The Divine Thinking 'engenders a power apt to the realization of its Thought' – apt, that is, to 'Creation'; this engendered power is the Third Hypostasis of the Divine Triad.

7.2 THE NUMERICAL SIGNIFICANCE OF 'B'

The relationship between the master of the universe—The Total one—and the mother of creation is best described in musical terms. The relationship between Atam—the Total one—and his female image (being Isis) is like the relationship between a sound of a note and its octave note. Consider a string of a given length as unity sets it vibrating; it produces a sound stopping the string at its midpoint and setting it vibrating again. The frequency of vibrations produced is double that given by the whole string, and the tone is raised by one octave. The string length has been divided by two; and the number of vibrations per second has been multiplied by two: one half (1:2) creates its mirror opposite (2:1). This harmonic relationship is represented by Atam and Isis.

In ancient Egyptian thinking, Isis as the number two is the image of the first principle—the divine intellect.

Isis' relationship to Atam (being an image of Unity) is the Octave that encompasses all the notes within it—the Womb.

Every number has one or more special properties, meaning the particular qualities of the described object which nothing shares with it. A special property of two is that it is the first whole number.

Two symbolizes the power of multiplicity; the female, mutable receptacle, while Three symbolizes the male. This was the 'music of the spheres', the universal harmonies played out between these two primal male and female universal symbols of Isis and Osiris, whose heavenly marriage produced the child Horus.

Plutarch confirmed this Egyptian wisdom in *Moralia Vol. V*:

> *"Three [Osiris] is the first perfect odd number: four is a square whose side is the even number two [Isis]; but five [Horus] is in some ways like to its father, and in some ways like to its mother, being made up of three and two. And panta (all) is a derivative of pente (five), and they speak of counting as "numbering by fives".*

Chapter 8 : The 3rd Sphere/ Letter 'G'—The Generative Universal Soul

8.1 THE ROLE OF LETTER 'G' IN THE CREATION CYCLE

As we have seen earlier, the first act of creation is to conceive it—both intellectually and physically. Atam as THE ONE, or First Existent "develops" into The Divine Mind, or First Thinker and Thought being the letter 'B' as represented by Isis who conceived creation both metaphysically and physically.

In the sequence of orderly creation process, the mansion/letter 'B'—representing the Supreme Intellectual-Principle 'engenders a power apt to the realization of its Thought'(apt, that is to 'Creation'). This engendered power is the Third Hypostasis of the Divine-Triad. This third power is the Universal Soul—the third letter 'G'.

The Third Hypostasis of the Divine-Triad is, then, the ALL-SOUL, or UNIVERSAL SOUL or SOUL OF THE ALL—it is the eternal emanation and image of the Second Hypostasis, the Intellectual-Principle.

In the Ancient Egyptian texts, the Universal Intelligence Isis gave life to Osiris, the Universal Soul. Every stage of creation tends to engender an image of itself. It tends also to rejoin the next highest, of which it is itself a shadow or lower manifestation—for Isis is an image of the first principle, and her shadow is Osiris. In the orderly sequence of creation, it was the female principle Isis who, after conceiving the plan, gave life to it. As such, Isis is called:

The Bestower of Life.

The Lady of Life.

The Giver of Life.

Time is presented as the 'life' of the Soul, in contrast to Eternity, which is the mode of existence of Intellect. However, Soul is an entity that spans various levels of reality, and we find on occasion the highest aspect, at least, of Soul largely assimilated to intellect.

The relation of the Soul to the Intellect is like the relation of the light of the Moon to the light of the Sun. Just as when the moon becomes full from the light of the sun, its light becomes an imitation of the light of the sun in the same way as when the soul receives the effusion from the intellect, and its virtues become perfect and its acts imitate the acts of the intellect. When its virtues become perfect, then it knows its essence or self and the reality of its substance.

The Divine-Intellectual-Principle has two Acts—that of upward contemplation of The One and that of 'generation' towards the lower/next sphere, the All-Soul. Likewise the All-Soul has two Acts: it at once contemplates the Intellectual Principle and 'generates' in the bounty of its own perfection the lower possiblity.

In other words, we need to recognize the Leading Principle of the Soul, or the Celestial Soul, concentrated in contemplation of its superior, and the Lower Soul, called also the Nature-Looking and Generative Soul, whose operation it is to generate or fashion the lower; the material Universe upon the model of the Divine-Thoughts and the 'Ideas' laid up within the Divine-Mind.

The All-Soul is the mobile cause of movement as well as of Form.

Likewise, all Sufi writings relate the third letter 'G' to 'al Nafas', which means *Universal Soul*.

The first four mansions/sections of the Ancient Egyptian 'Leiden Papyrus J350' are missing. However, Sphere/Mansion of the Letter '<u>D</u>.'—being the 26th letter [3rd letter from the last 28th letter]—gives the mirror image of the third Mansion/Letter 'G', whereas in letter '<u>D</u>.' as we will see later, it describes the deactivation of the reunited Generative Soul.

8.2 THE NUMERICAL SIGNIFICANCE OF 'G'

A special property of three is that it is the first odd number, as was considered in Ancient Egypt and clearly spelled out in Plutarch's text in *Moralia Vol. V*:

> *"Three [Osiris] is the first perfect odd number: four is a square whose side is the even number two [Isis]; but five [Horus] is in some ways like to its father, and in some ways like to its mother, being made up of three and two. And panta (all) is a derivative of pente (five), and they speak of counting as "numbering by fives".*

Esoterically, because all numbers are to be regarded as divisions of unity, the mathematical relationship a number bears to unity is a key to its nature. Both three and seven are 'perpetual motion' numbers. Divided into unity, they divide infinitely.

$$1/3 = .33333...$$

$$1/7 = .1428571428571...$$

Both numbers are related to Osiris who as the Universal Soul represents the 'perpetual motion'.

The principle that makes life come from apparent death was/is called Osiris, who symbolizes the power of renewal.

Osiris represents the process, growth, and the underlying cyclical aspects of the universe. Therefore, he was also identified with the spirits (energies) of grain, trees, animals, reptiles, birds, etc.

Osiris represents the cyclical aspect of nature—the physical creation and its cycles of becoming and returning.

8.3 NAMES & MEANINGS OF LETTER 'G'

The 'names' associated with the third letter 'G' are also consistent with all the above cosmic roles.

- **Gimel** (not camel but **Gameel**) means *beautiful—like the moon*)

> The most frequently used epithet of Osiris in the Ancient Egyptian texts is *"The Beautiful Being/One".*

- **Gamma** as an Egyptian word means 'the sum/total of'. The number of the letter 'G' is three which, in addition to being the first odd number, is also indicative of plural—the sum/total of all.

- The Egyptian word **GaMA.** means 'to make one of the many' = *to gather together/addition*

- The Egyptian word '**GoMLaT**' means a sentence = unity of parts/words—one encompassing all

- The Egyptian word '**GaBaL**'—[not Gamal] means a mountain—which is the shape of that letter

- **G D** = new

    = grandfather/ancestor

The letter 'G' had taken the place of Z in the Latin alphabet. The letter 'Z' in the Egyptian ABGD alphabets is the seventh letter. As shown above only 3 and 7 are 'perpetual numbers' representing the cyclical principle of creation, Osiris. It was associated with Dionysus and with the idea of resurrection.

8.4 THE PRIMARY TRINITY ABG (THE ABC)

It is worth repeating here that there are several aspects to the creation cycle. The different aspects compliment and do NOT contradict each other. As an example, the roles of the neter (god) Shu and the netert (goddess) Tefnut with Atam do not contradict and/or substitute for the roles of Isis and Osiris with Atam in this aspect of creation, which is detailed in this book.

For more detailed analysis of the various aspects of the creation cycle, read *Egyptian Cosmology: The Animated Universe* by Moustafa Gadalla.

The Three Hypostases of the Supreme-Being are quite frequently spoken of collectively as one transcendent Being or one Divine Realm. Sometimes, even, where one of the Three is definitely named, the entire context shows that the reference is not to the Hypostasis actually named, but to the Triad collectively or to one of the two not named. Thus, where the All-Soul is specified in a moral connection, the reference may really be to The First or to The Good; and where the connection is rather intellectual than moral or merely dynamic, the All-Soul may be used as a comprehensive term for the Godhead with a real reference to the Second Hypostasis, to Divine-Mind.

Its three Hypostases (or, in modern religious terminology, 'Persons') are, in the briefest description:

'**A**' – THE ONE, or First Existent.

'**B**' – The DIVINE MIND, or First Thinker and Thought.

'**G**' – The ALL-SOUL, or First and Only Principle of Life.

They are distinctively different, but are derived one from the other.

The Triad is The Divinity and is Divine: the All-Soul. It is the expression of the outgoing energy of the Divinity as the Intellectual-Principle is the expression of the Godhead's self-pent Thought or Vision.

In the Ancient Egyptian texts, the primary trinity begat all beings in the universe. This triad of '**ABG**' ensured a continuous relationship between the Creator and everything subsequent created.

The order of the primary triad is Being before Intellect and Intellect before Life, i.e.:

A – Being,

B – Intellect,

G – Life.

To know your ABG of the Creation Cycle is like knowing your ABC in a (Latin) language.

Chapter 9 : The 4th Sphere/ Letter 'D'—The Orderly Plan

9.1 THE ROLE OF LETTER 'D' IN THE CREATION CYCLE

The first group of trio letters 'A', 'B' and 'G' [1, 2 & 3] represents the Primary Trinity of the creation cycle.

From the Primary Trinity emanated two consecutive trio groups in order to complete the works of the First Conceiving Ennead/ Phase of Creation. being six acts of creation.

The group of trio letters 'D', 'H' and 'W' [4, 5 & 6] deals with the bringing forth of the attributes of the Creator that will act as the governors and administrators of the physical world—the Creation of the Celestial Government, as follows:

– 4th letter ' D' sets the Divine Creation Order and Administrative Plan.

– 5th letter 'H' connects the Creator [#1] to the Divine Order Plan of the 4th letter 'D'.

– 6th letter 'W' connects the Divine Intellect [#2] to the Divine Order Plan of the 4th letter 'D'.

The first of this group is the sphere/letter 'D'[#4] which sets the unifying holistic Divine Law to govern and maintain the natural working order of the created universe and sets the working relationship between its parts within a unifying orderly system/ matrix.

The first act of creation, which corresponds to the 4th sphere, is the framing of the Divine Laws, Maat, that will govern the physical world and the psyche of Man. Other components of Divine Law set the Interrelationship and Interdependence aspects.

Sufi writings echoe this Ancient Egyptian understanding by calling it 'tabi'at-i kull' meaning the *Universal Nature*—the holistic 'hidden' orderly plan of Uni-celestial government.

The first four [lunar] mansions/spheres of the J350 Leiden Papyrus are missing. However the mansion/sphere of the Letter '<u>Dh</u>'—being the 25th letter [4th letter from the last 28th letter]—gives the mirror image of the fourth Mansion/Letter 'D', wherein letter '<u>Dh</u>' (as we will see later) describes the realization of the unifying holistic basis of the workings of nature, Divine Law.

9.2 THE NUMERICAL SIGNIFICANCE OF 'D'

A special property of four is that it is the first perfect square. We say that four [D] is the first perfect square because it is the product of two multiplied by itself, and any number which is multiplied by itself is a (square) root and the product is a perfect square.

The "four corners" signify The Law.

[More about the mystical aspects of the number four in *Egyptian Cosmology: The Animated Universe* by Moustafa Gadalla.]

9.3 NAMES & MEANINGS OF LETTER 'D'

Several names are associated with the fourth letter 'D' and they all make sense in the Ancient Egyptian context of cosmic knowledge.

– DaL — as a verb means to guide/explain/show the way/.

– DaLeeL—means a Guide, ordination, process manual.

– DaLYLat—means Divine Laws—Physics—PHYSICALITY.

– DeLihLa—means 'to guide me when I am lost'.

– DoNYa—means Universe.

– DYN—means religion in its sense of setting the divine law of interrelationships.

9.4 THE TOP FOUR UNIVERSAL BEINGS—ABGD

There is an important distinction to be made about the first 4 numbers. The numbers 1 to 4 contain in themselves all numbers, since 1+2+3+4 = 10, while other numbers are compound.

Four terms are needed to account for the principle or idea of 'substance'. Five terms are needed to account for 'creation'and for the act of becoming, the event which will come next.

Chapter 10 : The 5th Sphere/Letter 'H'—The Divine Infusion

10.1 THE ROLE OF LETTER 'H' IN THE CREATION CYCLE

The first group of trio letters, 'A', 'B' and 'G' [1, 2 & 3], represents the primary Trinity of the creation cycle.

The second group of trio letters 'D', 'H' and 'W' [4, 5 & 6] deals with the setup for establishing and maintaining order in the creation process, as follows:

    – 4th letter 'D' sets the Divine Creation Order and Administrative Plan.

    – 5th letter 'H' connects the Creator to the Divine Order Plan of the 4th letter 'D'.

    – 6th letter 'W' connects the Divine Intellect to the Divine Order Plan of the 4th letter 'D'.

The previous chapter dealt with the 4th sphere/letter being the letter 'D', which sets the Universal Law & Order within a unifying orderly system/matrix.

The second and third acts of the trio letters 'D', 'H' and 'W'[4, 5 & 6]—being the 5th and 6th letters 'H' and 'W'- deals with Connectivity, but both also are intimately connected to each other; as 'H-W'.

This chapter deals with the 5th letter 'H'. In the following chapter we will focus on the 6th letter 'W' and then go on the intimate connection between the 'twin letters' 'H-W'.

The fifth mansion/letter 'H' represents the infusion of the divine essence into the planned order of creation which was set by the previous act of creation. As such it is shown in numerical terms as being 1+4—the number 1 ['A' The Alpha] infusing the 4th letter 'D' representing the orderly plan of creation.

This was described in the Sufi writings of the Egyptian Ibn Sina as "al-Bari' (bi'l-idafah)" meaning "Creator in relation to what is below it".

The 5th Letter 'H' accounts for 'creation'; for the act of becoming, the event. It is the Letter that conceives, quickens, develops and brings forth all things perceived and set forth by The Holy Spirit.

ALL aspects of the fifth sphere/letter 'H', as shown throughout this chapter, are found in poetic format in the fifth stanza of the Ancient Egyptian Papyrus entitled Leiden Papyrus J350—MaN-ZaLat (Lunar Mansion) no. 5.

10.2 THE SOUND AND WRITING FORM SIGNIFICANCE

– Consistent with its connectivity function, this fifth letter is pronounced in the Egyptian (and, by extension, other "Semitic" languages) in a DOUBLE form as 'HeH' with TWO 'H' sounds. Additionally, it is also written to affirm its connectivity function between the TWO Horizons, like the number 8 with a horizontal line dividing it into a circle above and a circle below the HORI-ZON-tal line.

– The horizon is a symbol of the dividing line between the waking consciousness, symbolized by the visible world by day, and the subconscious realm, symbolized by the night.

-The fifth Letter 'Heh' in Egypt is double in its shape—from the divine comes essence; from the created universe comes worship.

-The sound character of the fifth letter 'Heh' as aspirate, being a breathing sound, is singularly spiritual.

– The double emphasizes its CONNECTIVITY, continuity and its infinity, and expresses the character of The Deity, representing the creative principle, the giving of balance or life.

10.3 THE NUMERICAL SIGNIFICANCE OF 'H'

A special property of five is that it is the first recurrent number, also called 'spherical'. This is consistent with its shape/form—being two circles above and below the horizon. To write the number five one half the letter 'HeH' is needed, namely, one of the two circles exactly as is written in today's "Arabic" language.

Five is the first recurrent number because when it is multiplied by itself, it returns to itself; and if that number is multiplied by itself, it again returns to its essence – and so on forever. So, for example, five times five is twenty-five, and if this number is multiplied by itself, the product is six hundred and twenty-five, and if this number is again multiplied by itself, the product is 390.625, and if this number is multiplied by itself, the product is another number ending in twenty-five. Five conserves itself and whatever derives from it eternally, whatever it may reach. Five, as such, may also be called the first 'universal' number.

The significance and function of number five, in Ancient Egypt, was confirmed by Plutarch when speaking of Horus as the representative of this sacred number in his *Moralia, Vol. V*:

> **"And panta (all) is a derivative of pente (five), and they speak of counting as "numbering by fives".**

The number 'five' is considered the most important number in mathematics, philosophy, and music.

Both the number five and the typical Egyptian five-pointed star (the symbol of destiny) are associated with Horus. Horus represents the mediator between the earthly existence and the Divine. He is always portrayed in Ancient Egyptian depictions as the mediator presenting the deceased to his "Father in Heaven" Osiris.

Horus (like the Biblical Jesus) represents the 'Living god' on earth. He is the Heir, so to speak.

In the Egyptian symbolism of the four elements (water, air, earth and fire), Horus represents the element of air which in Egyptian is called 'HaWa', beginning with the letter 'H'.

Since the 5th Letter 'H' accounts for *creation', for the act of becoming, the event,* it will serve as an important unit/block throughout the creation cycle.

Chapter 11 : The 6th Sphere/Letter 'W'—Connectivity Between Upper and Lower Realms

11.1 THE ROLE OF LETTER 'W' IN THE CREATION CYCLE

The first group of trio letters 'A', 'B' and 'G' [1, 2 & 3] represents the primary Trinity of the creation cycle.

The second group of trio letters 'D', 'H' and 'W' [4, 5 & 6]—deals with the setup for establishing and maintaining order in the creation process, as follows:

– 4th letter ' D' sets the Divine Creation Order and Administrative Plan.

– 5th letter 'H' connects the Creator to the Divine Order Plan of the 4th letter 'D'.

– 6th letter 'W' connects the Divine Intellect to the Divine Order Plan of the 4th letter 'D'.

The previous chapter dealt with the 5th mansion/letter 'H' represents the infusion of the divine essence into the planned order of creation which was set by the previous act of creation. The Letter 'H' accounts for 'creation'; for the act of becoming, the event.

The 6th mansion/letter 'W' represents the connection between the divine thought/intelligence from the upper to the lower realms of the world. As such it is shown in numerical terms as [2+4]—the number 2 ['B'] intellect + the 4th letter 'D' representing the orderly plan of creation.

ALL aspects of the 6th sphere/letter 'W' are found in poetic for mat in the 6th stanza of the Ancient Egyptian Papyrus Leiden Papyrus J350. The stanza highlights its particular role in creation, numerical value, etc. in referring to:

– Connectivity between upper and lower realms

– Connectivity between two circles ["oceans"] which is the shape/form of the 6th letter 'WaW'

– Human offerings are made to get close/connect to the Divine—act of connectivity between lower and upper realms

So many of the words in this stanza begin with or include the letter 'W', such as:

'W' (world) = earth = whole world

'W'—as a prefix, it means *the oneness of /a unity of* [districts/regions]

'W'—as a suffix, it means *plural of*

'WaS.L' means *receipt* as well as *Connectivity/joining*

'WaS.aL'—as a verb—means arrive/arrival

'WaW'—means *and/with/together with*

'WaS.T.a'—means *connection*

'WaS.T.'—means *middle/in between/mediate*

11.2 THE SOUND AND WRITING FORM SIGNIFICANCE

– Consistent with its connectivity function, this 6th letter in pronounced in the Egyptian (and by extension, other "Semitic" languages) in a DOUBLE form 'WaW', with TWO 'W' sounds. Additionally, it is also written to affirm its connectivity function; like the number 8 turned 90 degrees with a vertical line dividing it into a circle next to another circle.

– 'WaW' as a word means *and/with/together with,* and is considered to be the image of mystery most profound and most incomprehensible, the symbol of the knot that unites.

11.3 THE NUMERICAL SIGNIFICANCE OF 'W'

A special property of the number six is that it is the first perfect number; i.e. if the divisors of a number add up to itself, it is called a perfect number, and six is the first of them. Six has a half which is three, and a third which is two, and a sixth which is one; and if these divisors are added up, the sum is equal to six.

The number 6 is not self-continuing, as five is. Its prolongation is 6 36 1296. Six times six is thirty-six; six returns to itself, and thirty appears. When thirty-six is multiplied by itself, the product is 1296 – six again appears, but not thirty. So it is evident that six conserves itself, but not what is derived from it. But five conserves itself (and what derives from it) eternally and forever.

[More about the significant of the number 'six' in *Egyptian Cosmology: The Animated Universe* by Moustafa Gadalla.]

Chapter 12 : The 7th Sphere/Letter 'Z'—The Plan of Separation

12.1 THE ROLE OF LETTER 'Z' IN THE CREATION CYCLE

We have seen that the first group of trio letters 'A', 'B' and 'G' [1, 2 & 3] represents the primary Trinity of the creation cycle.

We have also seen that the second group of trio letters 'D', 'H' and 'W' [4, 5 & 6] deals with the setup for establishing and maintaining order in the creation process, as follows:

– 4th letter ' D' sets the Divine Creation Order and Administrative Plan.

– 5th letter 'H' connects the Creator to the Divine Order Plan of the 4th letter 'D'.

– 6th letter 'W' connects the Divine Intellect to the Divine Order Plan of the 4th letter 'D'.

The previous chapter dealt with the 6th mansion/letter 'W', representing the connection between the divine thought/intelligence from the upper to the lower realms of the world.

As such it is shown in numerical terms as 2+4—the number 2 ['B'] intellect + the 4th letter 'D' representing the orderly plan of creation.

The third group of trio letters 'Z', '<u>H</u>.' and '<u>T</u>.' [7, 8 & 9], deals with creating Physical entities and Events and establishing the co-factors of life-forms as the foundation for the world; as follows:

– 7th letter ' Z'—represents the visual [mental] creation of the separated entities of the universe like these separation outlines in a connected picture puzzle.

– 8th letter '<u>H</u>.'—represents the means by which the separated entities of the universe continue to maintain their bond/contact/connection with their divine origin through a covenant setting the rules governing the correlations between the metaphysical and physical realms [the above and below].

– 9th letter '<u>T</u>.'—represents the culmination/outcome of assimilating the influences from the preceding spheres—the matrix within which all these functions operate simultaneously—to create the primordial forms of physical beings of the world: mineral, plant, animal, etc.

Our main topic here is the 7th mansion/letter 'Z', representing the visual [mental] creation of the separated entities of the universe like these separation outlines in a connected picture puzzle—an orderly separation plan.

The 7th sphere of the creation sequence represents the creation stage of the designs of the various species of being by first creating images which act as matrices or molds or "wombs" or "containers" or "funnels" that direct the flow of the forces of nature in their work of organizing physical matter into objects. (In other words: forming images of the Total Reality in order to create them.)

Whether we realize it or not, we use our imagination to shape our behavior and our destiny.

What is seen through this faculty are images of reality itself.

ALL aspects of the 7th sphere/letter 'Z' are found in poetic format in the 7th stanza of the Ancient Egyptian Papyrus of Leiden Papyrus J350. It is an extensive text. The German translator interpreted most of the text in a confusing, simultaneous combination of "local geographical places" and cosmic/spiritual settings! It talks about creative visualization – i.e., creating images of the separated entities of the universe symbolized by the divine vision of the eyes:

> *The marvelous (splendid, magnificent) creation of the Lord (Master) of everything (and everybody), came alive in the divine eye of Atam, the eye of Re."*

It also refers to the separated entities of the universe in an orderly separation/creation plan:

> *The parts were separated (broken up, loosened, created) by sword..."*

As a further confirmation of the aspects of creation mentioned above, we should note that the text for the reverse stage towards Reunification—being the 22nd mansion/letter 'T', as we will see later, describes *'TaW-H.eed'—Reunification*—which is opposite to separation.

12.2 THE NUMERICAL VALUE OF LETTER 'Z'

The universe is constructed in accordance with the nature of numbers. The number seven [Z] is the first complete number because seven combines in itself the meanings of all the (preceding) numbers; for all the numbers are even or odd, Two is the first even number, and four is the second; three is the first odd number, and five is the second. If the first odd number is added to the second even number, or the first even number is added to the second odd number, the sum is seven. So, if you add two, the first even number, to five, the second odd number, the sum is seven; similarly, if you add three (which is the first odd number) to four (which is the second even number), the sum is seven. And if one, which is the source of all numbers, is taken with six, which is a perfect number, the sum is seven, which is a complete number. This is their table: 1 2 3 4 5 6 7. This is a special property of seven which no other number before seven possesses.

The numbers 7, 9, 12, 28 are the first numbers that are called complete, odd square, exceeding, and perfect, respectively. Also, the cause of the exclusivity of those numbers comes, on the one hand, from the fact that $7 = 3 + 4$; $12 = 3 \times 4$; $28 = 7 \times 4$; and on the other hand, $7 + 12 + 9 = 28$.

Esoterically, because all numbers are to be regarded as divisions of unity, the mathematical relationship a number bears to unity is a key to its nature. Both three and seven are 'perpetual motion' numbers. Divided into unity, they divide infinitely:

$$1/3 = .33333\ldots$$

$$1/7 = .1428571428571\ldots$$

[For more information about the mystical aspects of the number seven, read *Egyptian Cosmology: The Animated Universe* by Moustafa Gadalla.]

Chapter 13 : The 8th Sphere/Letter 'H.'—The Covenant Rules

13.1 THE ROLE OF LETTER 'H.' IN THE CREATION CYCLE

We have seen that the first group of trio letters 'A', 'B' and 'G'—[1, 2 & 3] represents the primary Trinity of the creation cycle.

We have also seen that the second group of trio letters 'D', 'H' and 'W'—[4, 5 & 6]—deals with the setup for establishing and maintaining order in the creation process.

Now the third group of trio letters 'Z', 'H.' and 'T.'—[7, 8 & 9]—deals with creating Physical entities and Events and establishing the co-factors of life-forms as the foundation for the world, as follows:

– 7th letter ' Z'—represents the visual [mental] creation of the separated entities of the universe like these separation outlines in a connected picture puzzle.

– 8th letter 'H.'—represents the means by which the separated entities of the universe continue to maintain their bond/contact/connection with their divine origin through a covenant setting the rules governing the correlations between the metaphysical and physical realms [the above and below].

– 9th letter '<u>T</u>.'—represents the culmination/outcome of assimilating the influences from the preceding spheres—the matrix within which all these functions operate simultaneously—to create the primordial forms of physical beings of the world: mineral, plant, animal, etc.

In this chapter, our attention will be upon the 8th mansion/letter '<u>H</u>.' that represents the means by which the separated entities of the universe continue to maintain their bond/contact/connection with their divine origin through a covenant setting the rules governing the correlations between the metaphysical and physical realms [the above and below].

The 8th sphere of the creation sequence sets the boundaries and governing laws of relationships and interaction between the divine and the created universe—the right beliefs and practices—through the use of affirmation.

ALL aspects of the 8th sphere/letter '<u>H</u>.' are found in poetic format in the 8th stanza of the Ancient Egyptian's Leiden Papyrus J350. The 8th Stanza describes the interaction between humans and the divine powers during the prescribed festivals. The people provide rituals, sacrifices and offerings—the fruit of their labors—and the divine powers give back their blessing. This exchange is prominently depicted in all Ancient Egyptian temples.

So many of the words in this stanza begin with or include the letter '<u>H</u>.' such as:

<u>H</u>.aMaL = to carry. Its derivative is MaH.MaL = (The Holy) barque

<u>H</u>.aRM = holy/sacred

<u>H</u>.MuNu = the number eight

H. Q = chief/king

H.aD = boundaries/limits/laws

H. aT. = put down/set rules

H. eT = temple, shrine, house

H. eB = festival

H. e N = king/priest

H. Q a T = measure/gallon

H. S B = count, right order,reckon

13.2 THE NUMERICAL SIGNIFICANCE OF LETTER 'H.'

Eight [H.] is the first perfect cube because of the following argu-
ment:If any number is multiplied by itself, it is called a (square)
root and the product of two of them is a perfect square, as we
explained before. But if the perfect square is multiplied by its
(square) root, the product is called a perfect cube. Two is the first
number, and if it is multiplied by itself, the product is four, which
is the first perfect square. Then the perfect square is multiplied
by its (square) root, which is two, and the product is eight. Hence,
eight is the first perfect cube.

Eight is the first solid number because there can not be a solid
body without interlocked surfaces and there can not be a surface
without mutually adjoining lines and there can not be a line
without ordered points. The shortest line consists of two points,
and the narrowest surface consists of two lines, and the smallest
solid body consists of two surfaces; so the conclusion from these
premises is that the smallest solid body has eight parts. One of
them is a line which has two parts. If a line is multiplied by itself,
they form a surface which has four parts, and if the surface is
multiplied by one of its lengths, it will have depth from it, so then

there will be eight parts in all: two of length, two of width, and two of depth.

[More about the mystical aspects of the number eight can be found in *Egyptian Cosmology: The Animated Universe* by Moustafa Gadalla.]

Chapter 14 : The 9th Sphere/Letter 'T.'—The Primordial Forms of the World

14.1 THE ROLE OF LETTER 'T.' IN THE CREATION CYCLE

We have seen that the first group of trio letters A, B and G [1, 2 & 3] represents the primary Trinity of the creation cycle.

We have also seen that the second group of trio letters D, H and W [4, 5 & 6] deals with the setup for establishing and maintaining order in the creation process.

The third group of trio letters Z, H. and T. [7, 8 & 9] deals with creating Physical entities and Events and establishing the co-factors of life forms as the foundation for the world, as follows:

– We have seen that the 7th letter 'Z' represents the visual [mental] creation of the separated entities of the universe like these separation outlines in a connected picture puzzle.

– We have also seen that the 8th letter 'H.' represents the means by which the separated entities of the universe continue to maintain their bond/contact/connection with their divine origin through a covenant setting the rules governing the correlations between the metaphysical and physical realms [the above and below].

The 9th and last mansion/letter [of the Conception Phase], 'T.', represents the culmination/outcome of assimilating the influences from the preceding spheres—the matrix within which all these functions operate simultaneously—to create the primordial forms of physical beings of the world: mineral, plant, animal, etc. within a womb-like atmosphere, about to be manifested.

Herein ends the creation of the elements of the Noumenal world or division of the Objective realm. Herein also ends the establishment of order and the co-factors of life forms as the foundation for the world.

ALL aspects of the 9th sphere/letter 'T.' are found in poetic format in the 9th stanza of the Ancient Egyptian's Leiden Papyrus J350. This 9th Stanza describes the "assembly" of the nine members of the Grand Ennead to realize the outcome of their combined efforts in conceiving the primordial forms of physical beings of the world within a womb-like atmosphere; and about to be manifested.

So many of the words in this stanza begins or include the letter T., such as:

T. L A. = manifest or rise of sun

T.a BY A. a = nature = all images of God's truths [H.aQeQaT]

T.aR = fly

T.YR = birds

T.YF = light/invisible body—an image—Ka

14.2 THE NUMERICAL SIGNIFICANCE OF 'T.'

Nine [T.] is the first odd perfect square because three times three is nine and neither seven nor five nor three is a perfect square.

The numbers 7, 9, 12, and 28 are the first numbers that are called complete, odd square, exceeding, and perfect, respectively. Also, the cause of the exclusivity of those numbers comes, on the one hand, from the fact that 7 = 3 + 4; 12 = 3 x 4; and 28 = 7 x 4; and on the other hand, 7 + 12 + 9 = 28.

A human child is normally conceived, formed, and born in nine months; a fact which has a good deal to do with the role and importance attached to the number nine in Ancient Egypt. Correspondingly, the Company of Neteru (gods, goddesses) formed an Ennead, or group of nine, which caused the creation of man on earth. Number nine marks the end of gestation and the end of each series of numbers. If multiplied by any other number, it always reproduces itself (3 x 9 = 27 and 2 + 7 = 9 or 6 x 9 = 54 and 5 + 4 = 9, and so on).

Nine marks the transition from one scale (the numbers from 1 to 9) to a higher scale (starting with 10), and so it is the number of initiation, which is again similar to the birth of a baby after nine months.

PART III : THE ORDERLY
MANIFESTATION PHASE/
ENNEAD

Chapter 15 : The Theme of the Second Phase/Ennead

15.1 THEME OF THE PRIOR FIRST CONCEIVING PHASE/ENNEAD

The theme of the First Phase (1-9; Letters 'A' -'T.') is the objectification of a circumscribed area of undifferentiated energy/matter wherein the world will be manifested. It consists of the establishment of order and the co-factors of life forms as the foundation for the world.

Meditation on the sequence of the spheres from the top down reveals a gradual progression of qualities from the undifferentiated to the full differentiation of the tenth sphere being the beginning of the Second phase of the Creation Cycle.

The creation of the Universe, begins with the Creator and descends through the multiple states of Being, ending with the terrestrial creatures whose final link is man.

The First Phase leads to the second phase of the orderly manifestation of life forms in the created universe—that begins with the letter 'Y'.

15.2 THE THEME OF THE SECOND PHASE/ENNEAD OF ORDERLY MANIFESTATION

The Theme of the Second Phase/Ennead is the orderly manifestation of creation. This Second Phase deals with the creation of the noumenal and phenomenal planes, the two grand subdivisions of the manifested world. The letters of this Phase are therefore arranged in two groups of four letters, and the middle letter 'N' overlaps the two planes:

Y, K, L, M   N   S, '<u>A</u>', F, '<u>S</u>.'

The numerical values of the four letters of the Noumenal Plane are multiplications of the number 5. As explained earlier in the Fifth lunar mansion/letter, it accounts for 'creation'; for the act of becoming; the event. It is the Letter that conceives, quickens, develops, and brings forth all things perceived and set forth by The Holy Spirit.

The fifth mansion/letter 'H' represents the infusion of the divine essence ['A' The Alpha] into the orderly plan of creation [the 4th letter 'D'] that the divine essence [cosmic energies (neteru)] is found in ALL creations—in every stone, mineral, wood, etc.

As such, the number 5 serves as an important Unit/block throughout the creation cycle.

The numerical values of the four letters of the Noumenal Plane 'Y' through 'M' are associated directly with the 5th letter 'H'. The lunar mansions/letters of this Plane are multiplications of the number 5, as follows:

– 10th letter 'Y' is 5 x 2 with the numerical value of 10—**Universal Form**

– 11th letter 'K' is 5 x 4 with the numerical value of 20—**Universal Body**

– 12th letter 'L' is 5 x 6 with the numerical value of 30—**Divine Commandment**

– 13th letter 'M' is 5 x 8 with the numerical value of 40—**Divine Craftsmen**

Here ends the noumenal process of creation, to be followed by the orderly phenomenal manifestation process beginning at the 14th sphere/letter 'N'.

While the noumenal aspects are the results of the works of the mind, the phenomenal aspects are perceived by or perceptible to the senses, rather than the mind, and thus have at least an apparent external existence.

From this point [14th letter 'N'] until the end of The Manifestation Phase/Ennead, the spheres/letters will have the function of the 13th sphere/letter 'M' as its nucleus, as follows:

– 14th letter 'N' is 'M' + 'Y' [40 + 10]—with the numerical value of 50

– 15th letter 'S' is 'M' + 'K' [40 + 20]—with the numerical value of 60

– 16th letter '<u>A</u>.' is 'M' + 'L' [40 + 30]—with the numerical value of 70

– 17th letter 'F' is 'M' + 'M' [40 + 40]—with the numerical value of 80

– 18th letter '<u>S</u>.' is 'M' + 'K' + 'L' [40 + 20 + 30]—with the numerical value of 90

The nucleus sphere/letter, namely 'M'—being #40 (5 x 8) – deals with the manifestation of the divine shaping force to shape the various forms of the created universe.

This second phase/Ennead will lead to the third phase of Reunification that begins with the letter 'Q' (#100)—"the ASSEMBLY of all things in the plan of creation" which is compatible with the beginning of the Second Manifestation Phase, being sphere/letter 'Y' (#10) —"the plan of creation."

In the process of reading about each individual step/realm of this phase, the following points should be kept in mind:

1. Atam is the ONE and All one and; the Creation is the multiplication of his names and his forms, and this creation goes on forever.

2. In the Egyptian texts the neteru (gods, goddesses) are not personalities; they represent cosmic energies, as explained earlier. The names and symbols change their meaning, and a neter (god, goddess) at one given moment may symbolize quite another power at the next.

3. All "references" to "The Pharaoh/king" is actually to 'The Divine Man' or the divinity in man.

4. References to animals always represent animal symbolism at work: for example references to the baboon and that of the bull are both allusions to regained sexual power and fertility.

Chapter 16 : The 10th Sphere/Letter 'Y'—The Universal Form

16.1 THE ROLE OF LETTER 'Y' IN THE CREATION CYCLE

The ninth and last sphere/letter [of the Conception Phase/ Ennead] is the letter 'T.', which represents the culmination/outcome of assimilating the influences from the preceding spheres—the matrix within which all these functions operate simultaneously—to create the primordial forms of physical beings of the world: mineral, plant, animal, etc

Here the 10th lunar mansion/letter is 'Y'—being #10, which is the first of the Second Phase, The Manifestation Phase. It naturally begins with the unsealing of the overall plan of creation. It is the sphere/letter of the birth of the Universal Form of the primordial matter [like *a divine child*] after nine spheres (like human months) of childbearing internally, in the womb. The appearance of the primordial matter depends upon the Universal Form. Without form and shape, the primordial matter cannot become visible. The Universal Form comprises all forms and figures, which comprises everything that is in the spheres, the stars, and the mansions.

This 'Y' sphere—being #10 (5 x 2)—is intimately sourced to sphere/letter 'H' (#5).

ALL aspects of the 10th sphere/letter 'Y' are found in poetic format in the 10th stanza of this Ancient Egyptian's Leiden Papyrus J350. The 10th Stanza describes the unsealing of the overall plan of creation. It is the sphere/letter of the birth of the Universal Form of the primordial matter. So many of the words in this 10th Stanza begin with or include the letter 'Y', such as the prefix in verbs used to indicate the *coming forth* of the Universal Form of creation.

16.2 THE NUMERICAL SIGNIFICANCE OF LETTER 'Y'

The Grand Ennead emanates from the Absolute. The nine neters (principles) circumscribed about One (The Absolute) becomes both One and Ten. This is the symbolic analog of the original Unity; it is repetition, the return to the source.

Ten [Y] is the first number of the tens' rank, as one is the first number of the units' rank. It has another special property similar to a property of the number one; namely, that it only has one number adjacent to it, twenty, and ten is half of it, as we explained in the case of one, which is half of two.

The logarithm of 10 is One.

'Y' is a new One (log 10 = 1)

Chapter 17 : The 11th Sphere/Letter 'K'—The Universal Body

We have seen that the previous 10th sphere/letter 'Y—being #10 (5 x 2) – is the first of the Second Phase, The Manifestation Phase. It naturally begins with the unsealing of the overall plan of creation. It is the sphere/letter of the birth of the Universal Form of the primordial matter.

This now is sphere/letter 'K'—having the numerical value of 20 (5 x 4) – which is the second step of the Second Phase, The Manifestation Phase. Here we find the Universal Body being manifested in its structured heavenly constituents which move in an orderly manner in their designated courses and times. It represents the source of order for the pattern-maker.

This 'K' sphere, being #20 (5 x 4), like the previous sphere/letter 'Y' is #10 (5 x 2), is intimately sourced to the sphere/letter 'H' (#5).

ALL aspects of the 11th sphere/letter 'K' are found in poetic format in the 11th stanza of the Ancient Egyptian's Leiden Papyrus J350, where this 11th Stanza is entitled MaNZaLat (Lunar Mansion) Number 20. The text of

Stanza highlights its primary role of the Universal Body being manifested in its structured heavenly constituents, moving in an orderly manner in their designated courses and times.

Interesting and related utilizations of the letter 'K' in the Stanza are as follows:

KWeN = To form (by hand/palm)

taKWeeNoN = Formation/created forms

KoWN = the (Created Structured) Universe = THE UNI-VERSAL BODY.

K f i = uncover

Kaf/Kaff = uncover/make it plane/open/exposed

K M = complete/make complete

KoN = to be/enable

Chapter 18 : The 12th Sphere/Letter 'L'—The Divine Commandment

We have seen that the previous sphere/letter, namely 'K', with its numerical value being 20 (5 x 4), is the second sphere/letter of the Second Phase—The Manifestation Phase, representing the Universal Body being manifested in its structured heavenly constituents which move in an orderly nature in their designated courses and times. It represents the source of order for the pattern-maker.

Here we have the 12th sphere/letter; namely 'L', with its numerical value being 30 (5 x 6), as the third step of the Second Phase—The Manifestation Phase, which represents the Divine Commandment to ensure the control of the opposition forces of the manifested creation.

This sphere is the locus of manifestation of the overpowering Divine grandeur that ensures that the forces of light (order) can overcome and control the forces of darkness (disorder), the permanent enemy of the light.

The powers of this sphere are then able to bring distant things near, to make the invisible visible, to entrench faith in the heart, and to defend the world of mysteries against forces of darkness.

[For more information about the role of opposition in the creation cycle, read about Seth in *Egyptian Divinities* and/ or *Egyptian Cosmology*, both by Moustafa Gadalla.]

ALL aspects of the 12th sphere/letter 'L' are found in poetic format in the 12th stanza of the Ancient Egyptian's Leiden Papyrus J350, with its numerical value being 30. The text of the Stanza highlights the manifestation of the overpowering Divine grandeur that ensures that the forces of light (order) can overcome and control the forces of darkness (disorder)—the permanent enemy of the light—as represented by the Dragon Apophis and his allies such as the malicious liar.

Chapter 19 : The 13th Sphere/Letter 'M'—The Divine Craftsmen

We have seen that the previous sphere/letter is 'L', with its numerical value being 30 (5 x 6) as the third sphere/letter of the Second Phase—The Manifestation Phase, representing the Divine Commandment ensuring the control of opposition forces of the manifested creation.

Here we have the 13th sphere/letter; namely 'M', with its numerical value being 40 (5 x 8), as the fourth step of the Second Phase—The Manifestation Phase, representing the manifestation of the divine force shaping the various forms of the created universe.

This 'M' sphere—being #40 (5 x 8), like the previous three spheres/letters, is intimately sourced to the fifth sphere/letter 'H'.

ALL aspects of the 13th sphere/letter 'M' are found in poetic format in the 13th stanza of the Ancient Egyptian's Leiden Papyrus J350, with its numerical value being 40. The text of the Stanza highlights the manifestation of the divine force to shape the various forms of created universe. [For more information about the role of the neter (god) Ptah as The Divine Craftsman, read *Egyptian Divinities* by Moustafa Gadalla.]

———

This 13th letter 'M' is the last of four consecutive letters ['Y', 'K',

'L' & 'M'] which are intimately sourced to sphere/ letter 'H' (#5). Here ends the noumenal process of creation; to be followed by the phenomenal process, beginning at the 14th sphere/letter.

Chapter 20 : The 14th Sphere/Letter 'N'—Animating the Constituents of Creation

20.1 THE PHENOMENAL MANIFESTATION PROCESS

The noumenal process of creation consists of the first four spheres/letters [Y, K, L, M] of this Second Phase/Ennead, to be followed by the orderly phenomenal manifestation process, beginning at the 14th sphere/letter 'N'.

While the noumenal aspects are the results of the works of the mind, the phenomenal aspects are perceived by or perceptible to the senses, rather than the mind, and thus have at least an apparent external existence.

From this point [the 14th sphere/letter 'N'] until the end of The Manifestation Phase/Ennead, the spheres/letters will have the function of the 13th sphere/letter 'M' as its nucleus, as follows:

- 14th letter 'N' is 'M' + 'Y' [40 + 10]—with the numerical value of 50

- 15th letter 'S' is 'M' + 'K' [40 + 20]—with the numerical value of 60

- 16th letter '<u>A</u>.' is 'M' + 'L' [40 + 30]—with the numerical value of 70

– 17th letter 'F' is 'M' + 'M' [40 + 40]—with the numerical value of 80

– 18th letter '<u>S</u>.' is 'M' + 'K' + 'L' [40 + 20 + 30]—with the numerical value of 90

The nucleus sphere/letter – namely 'M', with its numerical value of 40 (5 x 8), deals with the manifestation of the divine force to shape the various forms of the created universe.

20.2 THE ROLE OF LETTER 'N' IN THE CREATION CYCLE

Here we have the 14th sphere/letter 'N' with its numerical value of 50 (M + Y). Here begins the combined manifestation of both the noumenal and the phenomenal process. This sphere/letter represents the twofold aspect of creation—the noumenal and the phenomenal—making spiritual forms pass over into bodily shapes that are connected with this sphere. This is the result of the combined aspects of:

– Sphere/letter 'M' with its numerical value of 40—being the manifestation of the divine force to shape the various forms of the created universe.

– Sphere/letter 'Y' with its numerical value of 10—being the development of the Universal Form of the primordial matter. The Universal Form comprises all forms and figures in the universe.

The appearance of the primordial matter depends upon the Universal Form. Without form and shape, the primordial matter cannot become visible.

The 14th sphere/letter 'N' mystically signifies the *'son of man'* – every being that is individualized and distinctive. Such was symbolized/represented in Ancient Egyptian texts as Horus, the offspring of the divine marriage of Isis and Osiris. The newborn is called 'Nu/Nunu' in the Egyptian language.

Since 'man' symbolizes/represents/replicates the universe, then (being a 'mini-universe') the offspring 'Nu/Nunu' represents this sphere/letter of the creation process.

ALL aspects of the 14th sphere/letter 'N' are found in poetic format in the 14th stanza of the Ancient Egyptian Leiden Papyrus J350, with its numerical value being 50. The text of the Stanza highlights the twofold aspect of creation of making spiritual forms pass over into bodily shapes. This is the result of the combined aspects of the manifested divine shapes of the various forms of the created universe and the Universal Form of the primordial matter, as explained above.

So many of the words in this stanza begin with or include the letter 'N', such as:

Nour = light

Nile = river

Nabat = plants

Nas = people

Nefer = beautiful

Nunu = offspring

N as a prefix = not/negation

N T / N W Y = water, flood

Neter = "god"

N e B = gold, all Lord, transform

Nesr = falcon

Chapter 21 : The 15th Sphere/Letter 'S'—Interdependence Activities Between the Above and the Below

We have seen that the previous 14th sphere/letter – namely 'N', with its numerical value being 50 (40 + 10), the twofold aspect of creation—the noumenal and the phenomenal—makes spiritual forms pass over into bodily shapes.

Here we have the 15th sphere/letter; namely 'S'—with its numerical value being 60 (40 + 20) – used to represent the second step in the combined manifestation of both the noumenal and the phenomenal process. This sphere/letter 'S' represents the upholding process of activities of interdependence between the Above and the Below through division of labor, rights and responsibilities, work, rituals and offerings in the prescribed festivals.

This sphere/letter 'S' represents the double relation between the various forms of creation [sphere/letter 'M'] and the orderly operation of the universe [sphere/letter 'K'].

This is the result of the combined aspects of:

– Sphere/letter 'M' being the manifestation of the divine force to shape the various forms of the created universe.

– Sphere/letter 'K' being the development of the 'Universal Body' that is manifested in its structured heavenly constituents which move in an orderly in their designated courses and times.

ALL aspects of the 15th sphere/letter 'S' are found in poetic format in the 15th stanza of the Ancient Egyptian Leiden Papyrus J350, with its numerical value being 60. The text of the Stanza highlights the upholding process of activities of interdependence between the Above and the Below through division of labor, rights and responsibilities, work, rituals and offerings in the prescribed festivals.

So many of the words in this stanza begin with or include the letter S, such as:

Swi = 60

Sawl = property

meSa<u>H</u>.aT = surveying

QaS = taking measurements

Assas = foundations

Setat = women

S M A = unite, (be) united

S N W = Two

SiR = official/noble

S D M = hear, obey

[More about the significance and the details of the Egyptian cosmic festivals in the book *Egyptian Mystics: Seekers of the Way* by Moustafa Gadalla.]

Chapter 22 : The 16th Sphere/Letter 'A.'—The Divine Overseer of the Created

We have seen that the previous 15th sphere/letter – namely 'S', with its numerical value being 60 (40 + 20) – represents the upholding process of activities of interdependence between the Above and the Below through division of labor, rights and responsibilities, work, rituals and offerings in the prescribed festivals. This sphere/letter 'S' represents a double relationship between the various forms of creation [sphere/letter M] and the orderly operation of the universe [sphere/letter K].

Here we have the 16th sphere/letter; namely 'A.', with its numerical value being 70 (40 + 30), representing the third step in the combined manifestation of both the noumenal and the phenomenal process. This sphere/letter 'A.' represents the double relation between the various forms of creation [sphere/letter 'M'] and the Divine Commandment to ensure equilibrium and balance—the necessary principles that reconcile order and disorder [sphere/letter 'L'].

This is the result of the combined aspects of:

– Sphere/letter 'M', being the manifestation of the divine shaping force to shape the various forms of the created universe.

– Sphere/letter 'L' as the Divine Commandment to ensure the control of the opposition forces of the manifested creation.

This sphere 16th sphere/letter '<u>A.</u>' is the locus of manifestation of the attributes of the Divine Overseer of the created being – omniscient, omnipotent, and omnipresent that protects and entrenches faith in the heart to defend the world of mysteries against the forces of darkness.

The most distinctive Egyptian symbol is the eye, which plays many complex and subtle roles. The eye symbolizes the following meanings:

<u>Omniscience</u>:—This term refers to the all-knowing nature of God. Webster defines it as "the quality of knowing all things at once; universal knowledge; knowledge unbounded or infinite." In short, God possesses superior knowledge and wisdom about everything, and that knowledge is all encompassing.

<u>Omnipotence</u>: —This term refers to the all powerful nature of God. Looking at Webster again, this is defined as "almighty power; unlimited or infinite power; a word in strictness applicable only to God." He is the all-powerful Lord who has created all things and sustains them by His Word.

<u>Omnipresence</u>: —This term that refers to the unlimited nature of God or His ability to be everywhere at all times. Relying upon Webster's, once again, we see omnipresence defined as "presence in every place at the same time; unbounded or universal presence; ubiquity."

ALL aspects of the 16th sphere/letter '<u>A.</u>' are found in poetic format in the 16th stanza of the Ancient Egyptian Leiden Papyrus J350, with its numerical value being 70. The text of the Stanza highlights the manifestation of the attributes of the Divine Overseer of the created being, omniscient, omnipotent, and omnipresent, that protects and entrenches faith in the heart to defend the world of mysteries against the forces of darkness.

So many of the words in this stanza begins or include the letter A., such as:

A. N Kh =life

A.aN = in help/action/assistance/activity

M A. = to pair/pair

A.YN = eye

A.eLaT = ailment

A.BYR = sweet breeze

A.DL = truth, justice

DoA.aA = prayer

A.DoW = rebellious

TaA.BaN = weary

Chapter 23 : The 17th Sphere/Letter 'F'—Multiplication of the Original Created Forms

We have seen that the previous 16th sphere/letter – namely '<u>A.</u>', with its numerical value being 70 (40 + 30) – represents the double relation between the powers of the Creator and the created. This sphere 16th sphere/letter '<u>A.</u>' is the locus of manifestation of the attributes of the Divine Overseer of the created being, omniscient, omnipotent, and omnipresent, that protects and entrenches faith in the heart to defend the world of mysteries against the forces of darkness.

Here we have the 17th sphere/letter; namely 'F', with its numerical value being 80 (40 + 40), repressneting the fourth step in the combined manifestation of both the noumenal and the phenomenal process. This sphere/letter 'F' represents the double relation between the various forms of creation [sphere/letter 'M'] and the descendants of the original created forms through multiplications and renewal.

ALL aspects of the 17th sphere/letter 'F' are found in poetic format in the 17th stanza of the Ancient Egyptian Leiden Papyrus J350 with its numerical value being 80. The text of the Stanza highlights the renewal/multiplication of the original created forms. References to the "bull" as sexual/generative powers and phallus are confirmation of the intent of this sphere/letter in the creation process. Also, the number 8 signifies the universal number of replication, as clearly found in a descending musical octave which is an image of the original tone, but at one half the vibration rate of the original note.

Chapter 24 : The 18th Sphere/Letter 'S.'—The Realized Manifested Coordinated Creation

We have seen that the previous 17th sphere/letter – namely 'F', with its numerical value being 80 (40 + 40), represents the double relation between the various forms of creation [sphere/letter 'M'] and the descendants of the original created forms through multiplications and renewal.

Here we have the 18th sphere/letter, the 'S.', with its numerical value being 90 (40 + 30 + 20) to represent the fifth and last step in the combined manifestation of both the noumenal and the phenomenal process as well as the ninth (and final) step in this Second Orderly Manifestation Phase/Ennead. This sphere/letter 'S.' represents the realization of the coordinated process of the manifested creation by forming images of the TOTAL reality. Such is confined to the perception of the external side of things, which limits its unifying function. In other words, it brings things together based on their external characteristics: this color with this other, this shape with this other, this personality type with this other, and so on.

This sphere/letter 'S.' represents the triple relation to spheres/letters 'M' + 'L' + 'K'—a trinity, to show that it is the sphere of digestion and integration. This is the result of the combined aspects of:

– Sphere/letter 'M', being the manifestation of the divine shaping force to shape the various forms of the created universe.

– Sphere/letter 'L'—being the Divine Commandment to ensure the control of the opposition forces of the manifested creation.

– Sphere/letter 'K'—being the development of the 'Universal Body' that is manifested in its structured heavenly constituents, moving orderly in their designated courses and times.

ALL aspects of the 18th sphere/letter 'S.' are found in poetic format in the 18th stanza of the Ancient Egyptian Leiden Papyrus J350, with its numerical value being 90. The text of the Stanza highlights the realization of the coordinated process of the manifested creation by forming images of the TOTAL reality through the integration of the triple spheres/letters 'M' + 'L' + 'K'.

So many of the words in this stanza begin with or include the letter S., such as:

S.aA.D = arise

S. H.A = awaken, came alive

S.oH.Bat = a group (with common interest/objective)

S.oWRat = picture/image

S.eFR = beginning, zero hour

S.aR(t) = turned into/became

S. B A. = fingers (toes)

S. B H. = Tomorrow/next morning

S̲.T = body

AS̲.L = Origin, original, point of beginning

S̲.aWaT = cackle, cry aloud, shout

S̲.A = Cackler, goose

S̲.AH. = shout

S̲.MT = silence, eternity

S̲.aDA = echo, cries (shouting) circulated

S̲.aDaQ = found the truth/REALITY

S̲.aFaa = clarity/purity

S̲.eFa(t) = attribute(s)

S̲.aLS̲.aLa = repeated sound

S̲. aA.D = rose climb

Herein ends the Second Phase/Ennead; being the orderly manifestation of creation in the noumenal and phenomenal planes—the two grand subdivisions of the manifested world.

PART IV : THE REUNIFICATION PHASE/ ENNEAD

Chapter 25 : The Theme of the Third Phase/ Ennead—The Reunification

25.1 THEMES OF PRIOR FIRST (CONCEIVING) AND SECOND (MANIFESTATION) PHASES/ENNEADS

The theme of the First Phase (1-9 'A' -'T.') is the objectification of a circumscribed area of undifferentiated energy/matter wherein the world will be manifested. It consists of the establishment of order and the co-factors of life forms as the foundation for the world.

This Second Orderly Manifestation Phase/Ennead (10-90 'Y' – 'S.') deals with the creation of the noumenal and phenomenal planes—the two grand subdivisions of the manifested world.

25.2 THE THEME OF THE THIRD PHASE/ENNEAD OF REUNIFICATION

The third phase is all about Reunification, which begins with the letter 'Q' (with the numerical value of 100)—"the ASSEMBLY of all things in the plan of creation"—which is compatible with the beginning of the Second Manifestation Phase (being the sphere/ letter 'Y' with the numerical value of 10)—"the plan of creation."

This is the Ascending Phase of The Joined Re & Osiris that leads to a NEW Alpha, Heru-Akhti of The Two Horizons.

The progression of the spheres/letters of this Reunification Phase, from sphere/letter 'Q' (with the numerical value of 100)

to that of 'Gh' (with the numerical value of 1000), is basically
the reversal of the progression from sphere/letter 'Y' (with the
numerical value of 10) to that of 'A' (with the "numerical" value of
1).

—

In the process of reading about each individual step/realm of this
phase, the following points should be kept in mind:

1. Atam is the ONE and All one and; the Creation is the multiplication of his names and his forms; and this creation goes
on forever.

2. In the Egyptian texts the neteru (gods, goddesses) are not
personalities; they represent cosmic energies, as explained
earlier. The names and symbols change their meaning, and
a neter (god, goddess) at one given moment may symbolize
quite another power at the next.

3. All "references" to "The Pharaoh/king" is actually to 'The
Divine Man' or the divinity in man.

4. References to animals always represent animal symbolism
at work—for example references to the baboon and that of
the bull are both allusions to regained sexual power and fertility.

Chapter 26 : The 19th Sphere/Letter 'Q'—Recall Assembly of Physical Beings

The previous 18th sphere/letter 'S.' represents the fifth (and final) step in the combined manifestation of both the noumenal and the phenomenal process. 'S.' is also the ninth and last sphere/ letter of the Manifestation Phase/ Ennead.

This 19th sphere/letter is 'Q', which holds the numerical value of 100. Here begins the end of the return process towards the original unity. This is the FIRST sphere/letter in the THIRD [and Final] Phase of the Creation Cycle—The Reunification Phase/ Ennead. It naturally begins with the assembly of all things in the plan of the Creator – in other words, the resurrection of all creation before the Creator.

This 'Q' sphere/letter—being #100—is intimately related to both the prior sphere/letter 'S.' (90), representing the combined manifestation of both the noumenal and the phenomenal process, and the Tenth sphere/letter 'Y' (#10), that represents the plan of the Creator.

In the complete orderly cycle of creation, the process of reunification must be the reverse mirror image of the First Phase of the Creation Cycle. As such, this 'Q' sphere/letter, being #100, is also intimately related to its reverse role in the process of creation—the tenth sphere/ letter 'Y' in more powerful way; for the 'Q' number of 100 is the second power to the number 10—sphere/letter 'Y'.

This 100th sphere/letter 'Q' represents the assembly of all the pieces of creation, as opposed to the tenth sphere/ letter 'Y' (#10) that represents the plan of the Creation.

—

ALL aspects of the 19th sphere/letter 'Q' are found in poetic format in the 19th stanza of the Ancient Egyptian Leiden Papyrus J350, with its numerical value being 100. The text of the Stanza highlights the assembly of all things in the plan of the Creator – in other words, the resurrection of all creation before the Creator. The resurrection of creation theme is also symbolized in the Stanza by using the 'resurrection eggs' metaphor.

The primary theme of the resurrection of creation is emphasized by using a 'Q' word— i.e. "QA/QaM" – very frequently in this Stanza.

QA/QaM = ascend, arise, come into being, to be high

Chapter 27 : The 20th Sphere/Letter 'R'—Recall Divine Creation Machinery

The previous 19th sphere/letter – namely 'Q'—is the FIRST sphere/letter in the THIRD [and Final] Phase of the Creation Cycle, The Reunification Phase/Ennead towards the original unity. It naturally begins with the assembly of all things in the plan of the Creator – in other words, the resurrection of all creation before the Creator.

This 20th sphere/letter – namely 'R'; having the numerical value of 200 (2Q) – represents the recall of the divine machinery [neteru (gods and goddesses)] that created the metaphysical images of creation of the physical beings of the assembled creation. In very simplistic terms, the prior sphere/letter 'Q' recalls the physical beings, and this sphere/letter 'R' recalls the metaphysical images ["souls"] of these physical beings.

In the complete orderly cycle of creation, the process of reunification must be the reverse mirror image of the First Phase of the Creation Cycle. As such, this 'R' sphere/letter—being #200 – is also intimately related to its reverse role in the process of creation—the ninth sphere/letter 'T.' that represents the hidden divine infrastructure, the machinery of the divine forces of the universe that created the primordial forms of physical beings of the world—mineral, plant, animal, etc.—within a womb-like (and about to be manifested) complete image within.

ALL aspects of the 20th sphere/letter 'R' are found in poetic format in the 20th stanza of the Ancient Egyptian Leiden Papyrus J350, with its numerical value being 200. The text of the Stanza highlights the recall of the divine machinery [neteru (gods and goddesses)] that created the metaphysical images of creation of the physical beings of the assembled creation.

Several words in this stanza begin with or include the letter

'R', such as:

RA./Re is the head of creation

RaS /ReS/ReSh = head, be wakeful/vigilant/…

Re-eS = Leader/head

ReMeT = humans/people—an Egyptian word that also means *teardrops of Re*

R e N = Real essence of a name

Chapter 28 : The 21st Sphere/Letter 'Sh'—The Authoritative Generative Trinity

The previous 20th sphere/letter, namely 'R', is the second sphere/letter in the THIRD [and Final] Phase of the Creation Cycle—The Reunification Phase towards the original unity. This returning sphere/letter 'R' represents the return of all things to the One, which is their principle and entelechy.

This 21st sphere/letter – namely '<u>Sh</u>'; having the numerical value of 300 (3Q) – represents the revelation of the Authoritative Trinity as the source of the divine forces of creation.

In the complete orderly cycle of creation, the process of reunification must be the reverse mirror image of the First Phase of the Creation Cycle. As such, this 'Sh' sphere/letter, being #300, is the mirror image of the 8th sphere/letter 'H.' that represents setting the rules governing the correlations between the metaphysical and physical realms [the above and below].

—

ALL aspects of the 21st sphere/letter 'Sh' are found in poetic format in the 21st stanza of the Ancient Egyptian Leiden Papyrus J350, with its numerical value being 300. The text of the Stanza highlights the revelation of the Authoritative Trinity as the source of the divine forces of creation.

Several words in this stanza begin with or include the letter 'Sh', such as:

<u>Sh</u> e <u>T.</u> = to gain possession of

<u>Sha</u>HaD = to wit

<u>Sha</u>f = to see through, reveal

<u>Sh</u> e N = circuit

Chapter 29 : The 22nd Sphere/Letter 'T'—Deactivating Generative Creation

The previous 21st sphere/letter – namely 'Sh'—is the third sphere/letter in the THIRD [and Final] Phase of the Creation Cycle, The Reunification Phase towards the original unity. This returning sphere/letter 'Sh' represents the revelation of the Authoritative Trinity as the source of the divine forces of creation.

This 22nd sphere/letter – namely 'T', having the numerical value of 400 (4Q), represents the deactivation of generative creation.

In the complete orderly cycle of creation, the process of reunification must be the reverse mirror image of the First Phase of the Creation Cycle. As such, this sphere/ letter 'T'—being #400 – is the mirror image of the 7th sphere/letter 'Z' that represents Creating Physical entities and Events; the separation of the creation pieces, mortality and the cycles of life and death.

The trio group of letters 'R', 'Sh' and 'T'—[200, 300 & 400] flow in opposite sequence to their counterparts in the First Conceptual phase/Ennead (being 'Z', 'H.' and 'T.' [7, 8 & 9]) that dealt with creating Physical entities and Events and establishing the co-factors of life forms as the foundation for the world.

ALL aspects of the 22nd sphere/letter 'T' are found in poetic format in the 22nd stanza of the Ancient Egyptian Leiden Papyrus J350, with its numerical value being 400. The text of the Stanza highlights the deactivation process of the generative aspect of the creation cycle.

Several words in this stanza begin with or include the letter 'T', such as:

TaW <u>H.</u>eeD = to become one—such as mating

TM/TMT = complete/to be complete/end

ToR = Bull

TaW = end

Tuat/Twat = "Underworld" (other world)

Chapter 30 : The 23rd Sphere/Letter 'Th'—Detaching Lower World

The previous 22nd sphere/letter – namely 'T'—is the fourth sphere/letter in the THIRD [and Final] Phase of the Creation Cycle, The Reunification Phase towards the original unity. This returning sphere/letter 'T' represents the deactivation of the generative creation.

This 23rd sphere/letter – namely 'Th', having the numerical value of 500, represents the elimination of the opposition forces that stand in the way of reunion with the Divine Origin, the forceful detachment from the lower [material] realm of the world and the triumph of mind over matter; so to speak.

In the complete orderly cycle of creation, the process of reunification must be the reverse mirror image of the First Phase of the Creation Cycle. As such, this sphere/ letter 'Th'—being #500 – is the mirror image of the 6th sphere/letter 'W' that represents the divine thought/intelligence's CONNECTION to the lower [material] realm of the world.

—

ALL aspects of the 23rd sphere/letter 'Th' are found in poetic format in the 23rd stanza of the Ancient Egyptian Leiden Papyrus

J350 with its numerical value being 500. The text of the Stanza highlights the elimination of the opposition forces that stand in the way of reunion with the Divine Origin—the forceful detachment from the lower [material] realm of the world with the symbolism of a bull whose Egyptian word starts with the letter 'Th'.

Chapter 31 : The 24th Sphere/Letter 'Kh'—The Pure Divinity

The previous 23rd sphere/letter, 'Th', is the fifth sphere/letter in the THIRD [and Final] Phase of the Creation Cycle—The Reunification Phase towards the original unity. This returning sphere/ letter 'Th' represents the detachment of the lower/creation/ material world in the way of reunion with the Divine Origin.

This, now, is the following 24th sphere/letter: namely 'Kh'—having the numerical value of 600, which represents the realization of the upper divine being, with its complimentary dual powers/ natures/attributes.

In the complete orderly cycle of creation, the process of reunification must be the reverse mirror image of the First Phase of the Creation Cycle. As such, this sphere/ letter 'Kh'—being #600 – is the mirror image of the 5th sphere/letter 'H' that represents the divine infusion in the planned order of creation (as opposed to separating the infused divinity from the lower world in this 24th sphere/letter).

—

ALL aspects of the 24th sphere/letter 'Kh' are found in poetic format in the 24th stanza of the Ancient Egyptian Leiden Papyrus J350, with its numerical value being 600. The text of the Stanza highlights the complimentary dual qualities/natures/ powers of the purely divine being.

Several words in this stanza begin with or include the letter <u>Kh</u>, such as:

<u>Kh</u>aLifa/<u>Kh</u>aDeM = benefactor

<u>Kh</u>aLQ = mankind/people/humankind/creation

Da<u>Kh</u>aL = enter

<u>Kh</u>oRM = hole

HoRa<u>Kh</u>TY = Horus of the two horizons

<u>Kh</u>aDaM = serve

A<u>Kh</u>et = the fertile field

<u>Kh</u>eBeR = he who comes into being—everything in existence.

<u>Kh</u>eRW = utterance/voice/sound

<u>Kh</u>aLaQ = [to] Create

Chapter 32 : The 25th Sphere/Letter 'Dh'—The Closing Decree

The previous 24th sphere/letter, 'Kh', is the sixth sphere/letter in the THIRD [and Final] Phase of the Creation Cycle—The Reunification Phase towards the original unity. This returning sphere/letter 'Kh' represents the realization of the upper divine being with its complimentary dual powers/natures/attributes.

This, now, is the following sphere/letter; namely 'Dh'. Having the numerical value of 700 represents the closing divine decree to conclude the ordained plan of creation.

This sphere/letter 'Dh' (#700) is the last of the group of trio letters 'Th','Kh' and 'Dh' [500, 600 & 700] recognizing the roles of the Celestial Government in the governing and administration of the created universe.

In the complete orderly cycle of creation, the process of reunification must be the reverse mirror image of the First Phase of the Creation Cycle. As such, this sphere/ letter 'Dh'—being #700 – is the mirror image of the 4th sphere/letter 'D' that sets the unifying holistic Divine Law to govern and maintain the natural working order of the created universe and sets the working relationship between its parts within a unifying orderly system/matrix.

—

ALL aspects of the 25th sphere/letter 'Dh' are found in poetic format in the 25th stanza of the Ancient Egyptian Leiden Papyrus J350, with its numerical value being 700. The text of the Stanza highlights the divine decree to conclude the ordained plan of creation. The stanza describes the assembly the divine forces for the last time to go over the original plan, discuss how it was executed successfully, and to issue the final decree to end this creation cycle

Several words in this stanza begin with or include the letter 'Dh', such as:

DhiKR = Eulogy, remembrance

MoDhaKeRat = transcription, decree (order, law), memorandum

DhaKar = remarked

Chapter 33 : The 26th Sphere/Letter 'D.'—Deactivating the Reunited Generative Universal Soul

The previous 25th sphere/letter, namely '<u>Dh</u>', is the seventh sphere/letter in the THIRD [and Final] Phase of the Creation Cycle—The Reunification Phase towards the original unity. This returning sphere/letter '<u>Dh</u>' represents the closing divine decree to conclude the ordained plan of creation.

This, now, is the following sphere/letter '<u>D.</u>'. Having the numerical value of 800 represents the integration all purified souls into the Generative Universal Soul—the Universe no longer lives and is silent and motionless.

In the complete orderly cycle of creation, the process of reunification must be the reverse mirror image of the First Phase of the Creation Cycle. As such, this sphere/ letter '<u>D.</u>'—being #800 – is the mirror image of the 3rd sphere/letter 'G', representing the Generative Universal Soul—the source of life and mortality.

The last group of trio letters, '<u>D.</u>' , '<u>Z.</u>' and '<u>Gh</u>' [800, 900 & 1000], represents the mirror image of the original Primary Trinity G, B and A [3, 2 & 1] of the creation cycle.

ALL aspects of the 26th sphere/letter 'D.' are found in poetic format in the 26th stanza of the Ancient Egyptian Leiden Papyrus J350, with its numerical value being 800. The text of the Stanza highlights the arrival and integration of all purified souls into the Generative Universal Soul where the Universe no longer lives, but is silent and motionless.

Several words in this stanza begin with or include the letter D., such as:

D. aNeeN = longing (yearning)

D.YaA = shinning

D.uat = Eternity, Under (hidden) world

Chapter 34 : The 27th Sphere/Letter 'Z.'—The One Consciousness

The previous 26th sphere/letter, 'D.', is the eighth sphere/letter in the THIRD [and Final] Phase of the Creation Cycle—The Reunification Phase towards the original unity. This returning sphere/letter 'D.' represents the integration of all purified souls into the Generative Universal Soul.

This, now, is the following sphere/letter; namely 'Z.'. Having the numerical value of 900 represents the state of consciousness. Since consciousness is immaterial, then it cannot be divided or multiplied. The consciousness that dwells in living things is the one undivided consciousness of the Supreme Being. Its appearance as separate and individuated conscious beings can be understood in the analogy of shining a light through different colored windows. The same light will come out on the other side with entirely different qualities as it shines through a yellow glass, a red glass, and so on. Thus, the One Consciousness comes out differently as it "shines" through men of different make-ups, dogs, horses, roses, worms, etc. Of "the form of things" in which the Supreme Being came into being, only one can afford the experience of Itself as God.

Herein ends the THIRD [and Final] Phase/Ennead of the Creation Cycle—The Reunification Phase/Ennead towards the original unity.

In the complete orderly cycle of creation, the process of reunification must be the reverse mirror image of the First Phase of the Creation Cycle. As such, this sphere/ letter 'Z.'—#900 – is related to the 2nd sphere/letter 'B' representing the Divine Intelligence that conceived Creation, the Image of the One.

The last group of trio letters 'D.', 'Z.' and 'Gh' [800, 900 & 1000] represents the mirror image of the original Primary Trinity G, B and A [3, 2 & 1] of the creation cycle.

The recovered Ancient Egyptian Leiden Papyrus J350 does not show any poetic texts for lunar mansions 900 and 1000. Some thought that they may have been torn out and lost, just like the first five stanzas of this Ancient Egyptian document, or that they were included on another papyrus that was never recovered. Another serious possibility should be considered, which is that the Ancient Egyptians never wrote about these last two spheres because their 'descriptions' are beyond our human existence—that ended by the sphere/letter D. [#800]—the deactivation of the Generative Universal Soul.

PART V : NEW ALPHA

Chapter 35 : The 28th Sphere/Letter 'Gh'—New Alpha

The previous 27th sphere/letter (namely 'Z.') is the ninth sphere/letter in the THIRD Phase of the Creation Cycle, The Reunification Phase towards the original unity. This returning sphere/letter 'Z.' represents the state of consciousness. Since consciousness is immaterial, then it cannot be divided or multiplied.

Herein ends the THIRD [and Final] Phase/Ennead of the Creation Cycle—The Reunification Phase/Ennead towards the original unity.

This, now, is the following sphere/letter; namely 'Gh', with the numerical value of 1000. Here is the LAST sphere/letter of the 28 lunar mansions, which is also a new beginning for a new cycle.

This returning sphere/letter 'Gh' is very similar to the sphere/letter 'Alef', where the sphere/letter 'Gh' means 'completion'—a godlike union with the Divine. The numerical number of the sphere/letter 'Gh'—being 1000 – confirms that it is a New Unity/New Alfa, since #1000 means *'Alf'* in Egyptian—a very slight vowel sound variation of the Original 'Alef'.

'Gh' is NOT the Original Unity 'Alef', but a replication like a musical octave's relationship to the Original Tone/Unity.

As a verb, 'Alef' means, in various contexts, "to unite, to join together, to grow, to tame, to go around in a cycle".

The numerical value of sphere/letter '<u>Gh</u>'—being 1000 – is the 3rd power of 10—The **Three phases of the Creation Cycle**.

1

SELECTED BIBLIOGRAPHY

Agrippa, Henry Cornelius. *Three Books of Occult Philosophy*. Montana, USA, 1992.

Ameen, Ahmed. *The Egyptian Customs, Traditions and Expressions*. Cairo, 1999 [Arabic text].

Arberry, Arthur J. *Sufism: An Account of Mystics of Islam*. London, 1956.

Assmann, J. *Agyptische Hymnen Und Gebete* (*Leiden Papyrus* p. 312-321). Zürich/Münich, 1975.

Baines, John and Jaromir Málek. *Atlas of Ancient Egypt*. New York, 1994.

Baldick, Julian. *Mystical Islam: An Introduction to Sufism*. New York and London, 1989.

Bleeker, C.J. *Hathor and Thoth*. Leiden, 1973.

Boylan, Patrick. *Thoth The Hermes of Egypt*. Oxford, 1922.

Breasted, James Henry. *Ancient Records of Egypt*, 3 Vols. Chicago, USA, 1927.

Budge, E.A. Wallis. *Egyptian Religion: Egyptian Ideas of the Future Life*. London, 1975.

Budge, E.A. Wallis. *The Gods of the Egyptians*, 2 volumes. New York, 1969.

Budge, Wallis. *Osiris & The Egyptian Resurrection* (2 volumes). New York, 1973.

Burke, O.M. *Among the Dervishes*. New York, 1975.

Cajori, Florian. *A History of Mathematical Notations, Vol. I.* Chicago, IL, USA, 1928.

Chejne, Anwar G. *The Arabic Language: Its Role in History*. Minneapolis, Minnesota, USA, 1969.

DeKerckhove, Derrick; and Lumsden, Charles J., eds. *The Alphabet and the Brain*. New York, 1989.

Diodorus of Sicily. *Books I, II, & IV*, tr. By C.H. Oldfather. London, 1964.

Drucker, Johanna. *The Alphabetic Labyrinth*. New York, 1995.

Egyptian Book of the Dead (The Book of Going Forth by Day), The Papyrus of Ani. USA, 1991.

El Hefni, Abd el-Menam. *The Sufi Dictionary*. Cairo, 1997 [Arabic text].

Ellis, Alexander John. *The Alphabet of Nature*. 1845.

Erman, Adolf. *Life in Ancient Egypt*. New York, 1971.

Erman, Adolph. *The Literature of the Ancient Egyptians*, tr. By Aylward M. Blackman. London, 1927.

Fadiman, James & Robert Frager, editors. *Essential Sufism*. San Francisco, 1997.

Fahim, Shadia S. *Doris Lessing: Sufi Equilibrium and the Form of the Novel*. New York, 1994.

Findlen, Paula, Ed. *Athanasius Kircher: The Last Man Who Knew Everything*. New York, 2004.

Firmage, Richard A. *The Alphabet ABECEDARIUM: Some Notes on Letters*. Boston, 1993.

Gadalla, Moustafa:
– *Ancient Egyptian Culture Revealed*, USA, 2007.
– *Egyptian Cosmology: The Animated Universe* – 2nd edition. USA, 2001.
– *Egyptian Divinities: The All Who Are THE ONE*. USA, 2001.

– *Egyptian Harmony: The Visual Music*. USA, 2000.

– *Egyptian Mystics: Seekers of the Way*. USA, 2003.
– *Egyptian Rhythm: The Heavenly Melodies*. USA, 2002.

– *Egyptian Romany: The Essence of Hispania*. USA, 2004.

Gardiner, Sir Alan. *Egyptian Grammar: Being an Introduction to the Study of Hieroglyphs*, 3rd ed. Oxford, 1994.

Gilsenan, Michael. *Saint and Sufi in Modern Egypt*. Oxford, 1973.

Godwin, Joscelyn. *Robert Fludd: Hermatic Philosopher and Surveyor of Two Worlds*. London, 1990.

Godwin, Joscelyn. *Athanasius Kircher: A Renaissance Man and the Quest for Lost Knowledge*. London, 1979.

Healey, John F. *The Early Alphabet*. London, 1990.

Herodotus. *The Histories*. Tr. By Aubrey DeSelincourt. London, 1996.

Kastor, Joseph. *Wings of the Falcon, Life and Thought of Ancient Egypt*. USA, 1968.

Menninger. *Numbers Words and Number Symbols*, Tr. by Paul Broneer, Cambridge, MA, USA, 1969.

Nicholson, Reynold A. *The Mystics of Islam*. New York, 1975.

Peacey, Howard. *The Meaning of the Alphabet*. Los Angeles, CA, USA, 1949.

Pendlebury, David, Editor (Tr. From Arabic by Nabil Safwat, Compiled by Abd al-Razzaq al-Qashani). *A Glossary of Sufi Technical Terms*. London, 1991.

Petrie, W.M. Flinders. *The Formation of the Alphabet*. London, 1912.

Piankoff, Alexandre. *The Litany of Re*. New York, 1964.

Piankoff, Alexandre. *The Pyramid of Unas Texts*. Princeton, NJ, USA, 1968.

Piankoff, Alexandre. *The Shrines of Tut-Ankh-Amon Texts*. New York, 1955.

Plato. *The Collected Dialogues of Plato including the Letters*. Edited by E. Hamilton & H. Cairns. New York, 1961.

Plotinus. *The Enneads*, in 6 volumes, Tr. By A.H. Armstrong. London, 1978.

Plotinus. *The Enneads*, Tr. By Stephen MacKenna. London, 1991.

Plutarch, *De Iside Et Osiride*. Tr. By J. Gwyn Griffiths. Wales, U.K., 1970.

Plutarch. *Plutarch's Moralia, Volume V*. Tr. by Frank Cole Babbitt. London, 1927.

Pritchard, James B., Ed. *Ancient Near Eastern Texts*. Princeton, NJ, USA, 1955.

Shafer, Byron E. (Ed.). *Religion in Ancient Egypt*. Ithaca, NY, USA, 1991.

Shah, Idries. *The Sufis*. New York, 1964.

Sicilus, *Diodorus*. Vol 1. Tr. by C.H. Oldfather. London.

Silverman, David and Torode, Brian. *The Material Word: Some Theories of Language and its Limits*. London, 1980.

Subhan, John A. *Sufism: Its Saints and Shrines*. Lucknow [pref. 1938].

Taylor, Isaac. *The History of the Alphabet*, 2 vols. New York, 1899.

Trimingham, J. Spencer. *The Sufi Orders in Islam*. New York, 1998.

Wilkins, John. *Mercury or the Secret and Swift Messenger*. London, 1641.

Wilkinson, J. Gardner. *The Ancient Egyptians: Their Life and Customs*. London, 1988.

Several Internet sources.

Numerous references in the Arabic language.

2

SOURCES AND NOTES

.The author is extremely knowledgeable in several languages, including the Egyptian and Arabic tongues.

References to sources in the previous section, Selected Bibliography, are only referred to for their facts, events, and dates—not for their interpretations of such information.

It should be noted that if a reference is made to one of the author Moustafa Gadalla's books, that each of his books contain appendices for its own extensive bibliography as well as detailed Sources and Notes.

<u>Chapter 1. Historical Deception of the (Ancient) Egyptian Linguistics</u>

The Hieroglyphics Smoke Screen: Gardiner [Egyptian Grammar]

The (Ancient) Egyptian Alphabetical Form of Writing: Taylor Vol.1, Plato, Erman [Literature...], Petrie [Formation...], Gadalla [Culture], Gardiner [Egyptian Grammar]

Egyptian is Dead—Long Live "Arabic": Gardiner [Egyptian Grammar]

The Real and "Fabricated" Sequence of the Alphabet: Baines, Budge [Rosetta Stone]

Egyptian Cosmology and Allegories: Gadalla [Culture], Godwin [Kircher]

Chapter 2. The Principles and Principals of Creation

The Egyptian Creation Accounts—Overview: Gadalla [Egyptian Cosmology, Divinities], Kastor, Budge, Wilkinson

In the Beginning: Practically all books agree.

The Energies of The Creation Cycle: Gadalla [Cosmology, Divinities, Mystics], Kastor, Budge, Wilkinson, Piankoff [all]

Chapter 3. The Cosmic Manifestation of The Egyptian Alphabet

The Formative Logos (Sound and Form): Gadalla [Cosmology, Divinities], Piankoff [Re]

The Cosmic formation of Alphabet: Bleeker, Diodorus, Gadalla [Divinities], Firmage, Plato, Plutarch, Peacey

The Lunar Manifestations of The Alphabetical Letters: Bleeker

The Sequence of the Creation Cycle: Practically all references.

Thoth and Seshat—Letters and Numbers: Gadalla [Harmony], Firmage, Fahim, Cajori

The Numerical Values of the 28 Alphabets: Firmage, Taylor, Vol.2

The Trilateral Stem Verb—Gametria: Gardiner, Gadalla [Romany], Rasula, Fahim, Drucker

Chapter 4. The Three Primary Phases of the Creation Cycle

Leiden Papyrus' 3 Tiers—Enumeration of The Three Phases: Assmann, Pritchard

The Three Primary Enneads of the Creation Cycle: Budge Gods I & II, Piankoff [all]

Litany of Re—Three Phases of Creation Cycle: Piankoff [Re], Budge Gods I &II

Sufism and Ancient Egyptian Three Phases Cycle: Gadalla [Mystics], Shah, Fahim

Chapter 5. The Theme of the First Phase/Ennead

Practically all references, particularly Piankoff [Re, Unas], Arabic references

Chapter 6. The 1st Sphere/Letter 'A'

Kastor, Piankoff [Re], Gardiner, Budge [Language], Gadalla [Cosmology & Divinities], Gadalla being an Egyptian native, several Arabic references

Chapter 7. The 2nd Sphere/Letter 'B'

Kastor, Firmage, Piankoff [Re], Gardiner, Budge [Language], Gadalla [Cosmology & Divinities], Gadalla being an Egyptian native, several Arabic references

Chapter 8. The 3rd Sphere/Letter 'G'

Kastor, Plutarch, Piankoff [Re], Gardiner, Budge [Language], Gadalla [Cosmology & Divinities], Gadalla being an Egyptian native, several Arabic references

Chapter 9. The 4th Sphere/Letter 'D'

Gardiner, Budge [Language], Gadalla [Cosmology & Divinities], Gadalla being an Egyptian native, several Arabic references

Chapter 10. The 5th Sphere/Letter 'H'

Assmann, Kastor, Plutarch, Gardiner, Budge [Language], Drucker, Gadalla [Cosmology, Divinities, Harmony & Rhythm], Gadalla being an Egyptian native, several Arabic references

Chapter 11. The 6th Sphere/Letter 'W'

Assmann, Kastor, Firmage, Gardiner, Budge [Language], Drucker, Gadalla [Cosmology & Divinities], Gadalla being an Egyptian native, several Arabic references

Chapter 12. The 7th Sphere/Letter 'Z'

Assmann, Kastor, Firmage, Drucker, Herodotus, Gardiner, Budge [Language], Gadalla [Cosmology & Divinities], Gadalla being an Egyptian native, several Arabic references

Chapter 13. The 8th Sphere/Letter 'H.'

Assmann, Kastor, Gardiner, Budge [Language], Gadalla [Cosmology & Divinities], Gadalla being an Egyptian native, several Arabic references

Chapter 14. The 9th Sphere/Letter 'T.'

Assmann, Kastor, Gardiner, Budge [Language], Gadalla [Cosmology & Divinities], Gadalla being an Egyptian native, several Arabic references

Chapter 15. The Theme of the Second Phase/Ennead

Practically all references, particularly Piankoff [Re, Unas], Arabic references

Chapter 16. The 10th Sphere/Letter 'Y'

Assmann, Taylor [Vol.I], Firmage, Drucker, Kastor, Gardiner, Budge [Language], Gadalla [Cosmology & Divinities], Gadalla being an Egyptian native, several Arabic references

Chapter 17. The 11th Sphere/Letter 'K'

Assmann, Taylor [Vol. I], Firmage, Drucker, Kastor, Gardiner, Budge [Language], Gadalla [Cosmology & Divinities], Gadalla being an Egyptian native, several Arabic references

Chapter 18. The 12th Sphere/Letter 'L'

Assmann, Kastor, Gardiner, Budge [Language], Gadalla [Egyptian & Divinities], Gadalla being an Egyptian native, several Arabic references

Chapter 19. The 13th Sphere/Letter 'M'

Assmann, Taylor [Vol. I], Firmage, Drucker, Kastor, Gardiner, Budge [Language], Gadalla [Cosmology & Divinities], Gadalla being an Egyptian native, several Arabic references

Chapter 20. The 14th Sphere/Letter 'N'

Assmann, Firmage, Kastor, Gardiner, Budge [Language], Gadalla [Cosmology& Divinities], Gadalla being an Egyptian native, several Arabic references

Chapter 21. The 15th Sphere/Letter 'S'

Assmann, Driver, Drucker, Cajori, Kastor, Gardiner, Budge [Language], Gadalla [Cosmology, Mystics & Divinities], Gadalla being an Egyptian native, several Arabic references

Chapter 22. The 16th Sphere/Letter 'A.'

Assmann, Pritchard, Driver, Drucker, Gardiner, Budge [Language], Gadalla [Cosmology, Harmony & Divinities], Gadalla being an Egyptian native, several Arabic references

Chapter 23. The 17th Sphere/Letter 'F'

Assmann, Pritchard, Gardiner, Budge [Language], Gadalla [Cosmology, Mystics & Divinities], Gadalla being an Egyptian native, several Arabic references

Chapter 24. The 18th Sphere/Letter 'S.'

Assmann, Pritchard, Gardiner, Budge [Language], Gadalla [Cosmology, Mystics & Divinities], Gadalla being an Egyptian native, several Arabic references

Chapter 25. The Theme of the Third Phase/Ennead

Practically all references, particularly Kastor, Budge [all], Piankoff [Re, Unas], Arabic references

Chapter 26. The 19th Sphere/Letter 'Q'

Assmann, Pritchard, Firmage, Drucker, Driver, Gardiner, Budge [Language], Gadalla [Cosmology, Mystics & Divinities], Gadalla being an Egyptian native, several Arabic references

Chapter 27. The 20th Sphere/Letter 'R'

Assmann, Pritchard, Firmage, Drucker, Driver, Gardiner, Budge [Language], Gadalla [Cosmology, Mystics & Divinities], Gadalla being an Egyptian native, several Arabic references

Chapter 28. The 21st Sphere/Letter 'Sh'

Assmann, Pritchard, Firmage, Drucker, Driver, Gardiner, Budge [Language], Gadalla [Cosmology, Mystics & Divinities], Gadalla being an Egyptian native, several Arabic references

Chapter 29. The 22nd Sphere/Letter 'T'

Assmann, Pritchard, Firmage, Drucker, Driver, Gardiner, Budge [Language], Gadalla [Cosmology, Mystics & Divinities], Gadalla being an Egyptian native, several Arabic references

Chapter 30. The 23rd Sphere/Letter 'Th'

Assmann, Pritchard, Kastor, Gardiner, Budge [Language], Gadalla [Cosmology, Mystics & Divinities], Gadalla being an Egyptian native, several Arabic references

Chapter 31. The 24th Sphere/Letter 'Kh'

Assmann, Pritchard, Kastor, Gardiner, Budge [Language], Gadalla [Cosmology, Mystics & Divinities], Gadalla being an Egyptian native, several Arabic references

Chapter 32. The 25th Sphere/Letter 'Dh'

Assmann, Pritchard, Kastor, Gardiner, Budge [Language], Gadalla [Cosmology, Mystics & Divinities], Gadalla being an Egyptian native, several Arabic references

Chapter 33. The 26th Sphere/Letter 'D.'

Assmann, Pritchard, Kastor, Gardiner, Budge [Language], Gadalla [Cosmology, Mystics & Divinities], Gadalla being an Egyptian native, several Arabic references

Chapter 34. The 27th Sphere/Letter 'Z.'

Kastor, Firmage, Piankoff [Re], Gardiner, Budge [Language],

Gadalla [Cosmology, Mystics & Divinities], Gadalla being an Egyptian native, several Arabic references

Chapter 35. The 28th Sphere/Letter 'Gh'

Kastor, Firmage 56-7, Piankoff [Re], Gardiner, Budge [Language], Gadalla [Cosmology, Mystics & Divinities], Gadalla being an Egyptian native, several Arabic references.

www.ingramcontent.com/pod-product-compliance
Lightning Source LLC
Chambersburg PA
CBHW060926140726
47996CB00001B/401